JOSEPH ATKINSON

Aki's Amusements

Essays on the Absurd and the Intimate

First published by Joseph Atkinson Press 2025

Copyright © 2025 by Joseph Atkinson

All rights reserved. No part of this publication may be reproduced, stored or transmitted in any form or by any means, electronic, mechanical, photocopying, recording, scanning, or otherwise without written permission from the publisher. It is illegal to copy this book, post it to a website, or distribute it by any other means without permission.

First edition

ISBN: 978-1-7644344-0-9

Cover art by Sebastion Dodds-Painter
Advisor: Albert Roggo

This book was professionally typeset on Reedsy.
Find out more at reedsy.com

Contents

Foreword From Albert Roggo v
1. Reflective Growth Through Repetition 1
2. The Bittersweet Symphony of Artistic Persistence 4
3. Polysecure Taught Me to Love Louder and Ask Softer 7
4. Cuddles, Chaos, and Consent: New Rules for Intimacy 10
5. bell hooks Said It Better: Her Feminism Is a Welcome Mat,... 14
6. The Absurdity of Extremes: Middleground in Heartbreak High 18
7. When Identity Becomes Everything: Finding Balance Again 22
8. Monsters in Thought or Action: Comparing Nightcrawler &... 24
9. Interpreting Masculinity: Character Analysis of 'The... 29
10. The Paradox of Influence: Navigating the Crossroads of Power... 32
11. Authenticity vs. Performance in Relationship Building: A... 35
12. Nonviolent Communication and the Choreography of Empathy 38
13. Buying Love: Spending and Romance 41
14. Quirky Hearts: Unconventional Love in 'Eagle vs Shark' 44
15. Laughing Through it All: The D&D Energy of Tactical Breach... 46
16. How Wildermyth Taught Me to Pretend 49
17. Demystifying the Deck: Why Card Games Are Having a Glorious... 52
18. Monster Train and Matrix Design 55
19. Peglin's Role in the Evolution of Hybrid Games 59
20. Rolling the Dice: The Tension and Transparency of Randomness... 62
21. The Joy of "Working" in Satisfactory 65
22. Redline: Burn Everything 70
23. This Is Not a Bar (But It Fucking Is): Surrealism Meets... 73

24 Life's a Joke, and Then You Cry: The Tragicomedy of Diary of...	76
25 Aussie Humor Through Fisk: The the Inner-City Comedians'...	80
26 The Grey of Apple Cider Vinegar	84
27 The Power of Distraction: How "Everything is Perfect" Keeps...	87
28 The Silent Backbone: How Sokka's Wit Shapes Avatar	91
29 Dune's Realpolitik of Religion	97
30 Treasure Planet: How a Trip to Space Saved an Old Story from...	101
31 Arrival and "Not Actually That Deep" Sci-Fi Films	104
32 Grounding Fantasy: Lessons from Delicious in Dungeon	108
33 Polishing the Past: Ethical Memoir Writing Explored Through...	114
34 The Role of Reader Engagement	117
35 The Quiet Revolution: How Thich Nhat Hanh Changed Spiritual...	124
36 The Enigmatic Cloak of Spiritual Science	127
About the Author	131

Foreword From Albert Roggo

In the visual arts, painting, architecture, sculpture, and beyond, it has been common practice to turn one's work upside down in order to literally re-view it. This allows the artist —who doubtless has stared at their piece for many hours with furrowed brow — to see it freshly, as for the first time. In doing so, suddenly and somewhat frighteningly, entirely new images can appear from the work. Great clumps of colour, once hidden by the artist's focused vision, can overwhelm the viewer's new perspective, rendering it unviewable. A delicate and carefully crafted figure may suddenly appear to be consumed by the background. Or, impressive new ideas, evocative and emotional, hidden only by the assumptions of the artist, may burst from the work. Just like the artist can while creating their work literally twist their canvas or their viewpoint to gather more and new information from a piece of art, the casual reader of a book, viewer of a movie, consumer of whatever piece of art, can make an effort to observe at an angle, and have that piece of art breathe new breath.

This technique is the backbone to many of Atkinson's essays in this collection. By refusing to interpret a product from the most obvious point of view, by pairing his analysis of one product with a seemingly disparate concept, he uncovers vast analytical meaning and emotional depth from a source that appears at first to be shallow. By example, look at his essay How Wildermyth Taught Me to Pretend. In rejecting the typical mandates of the reviewer (analysing mechanics or discussing 'game feel'), Atkinson is able to use his experience with Wildermyth to discuss and reflect on the childlike beauty of free-form storytelling. He sees how Wildermyth's approach to the emergent style of storytelling flows from as little as 'a pile of vague breadcrumbs, some quirks, some events, maybe a line of dialogue' and in capturing your imagination, draws your mind into spinning grand and emotional stories. And this small joy feels like one lost by many as they approach adulthood.

Another relevant technique is Ostranenie, or, defamiliarization. Coined by Soviet writer Viktor Shklovsky, it's a rather simple seeming idea: introduce a familiar concept in an unfamiliar way. By doing so, the audience, is forced to truly see what is being presented, rather than just recognising it. The runner-worn schoolyards and halogen-lit hallways of Heartbreak High are filled to the brim with the familiar-seeming people, locations, activities, and dramas native to school life. It is from this familiarity that Atkinson is able to draw up discussions on modern liberalism and conservatism and the limitations that these very concepts put on our own thinking: 'the mess society finds itself in cannot be tidied up with the broad strokes of liberalism or conservatism'.

We must ask ourselves now: why does it all matter? It is, of course, intellectually rewarding to spend some time producing a nuanced and interesting take on a movie, video game, or prestige TV show. But outside of cerebral pleasure, the practice may appear to be a somewhat pointless pastime. Yet perhaps it is the very pointlessness of the activity that holds its true value. By training ourselves to be able to peer into the art we consume at a sideways glance, we learn how to tilt our view of the world around us. We see beyond the assumptions that can be woven into our relationships, personal reflections, and senses of humour. In the familiar, we discover new tensions, hidden shapes, and, perhaps most importantly, whole possibilities we might otherwise ignore.

Perhaps from my description, this discipline of twisting your head and forcing your brain to recontextualise what you are seeing might seem somewhat dry – but there is a playfulness to Atkinson's process that acts as the engine of his analysis. His ability to laugh and wonder his way through topics as disparate as a food-based dungeon-crawling anime (see Grounding Fantasy: Lessons from Delicious in Dungeon), which becomes a dedication to the beauty of everyday interaction, to the inventiveness and innovations in publishing style of a Buddhist Monk (in The Quiet Revolution: How Thich Nhat Hanh Changed Spiritual Publishing) elevates what feels as if it should be a damp and dour activity. By twisting playfulness from an intellectual indulgence into an analytical method, we can bring to life this under loved endeavour. Fresh and free associations percolate naturally given this strategy, for, as Atkinson demonstrates, what is concealed by habit and convention can be uncovered through a simple sense of play.

At the end of the day, the value of Atkinson's essays lies not simply in the subjects he examines, but in the analytical stance he models for the reader. To approach art and culture askew, to flip the canvas, to tilt the frame, to force the ordinary to appear strange, is to resist the comfort of habit. It is to remember that one's perspective is never fixed, and that in the shifting of angles new truths may come into view. These essays, then, are not simply critiques of games, shows, or books, but demonstrations of how to keep one's analytical vision clear and fresh. They invite us to play, to defamiliarise and to invert. In so doing to glimpse more than what was first apparent. If we follow that lead, the reward is not merely seeing Atkinson's subjects differently, but glimpsing the world itself in shapes we had overlooked.

1

Reflective Growth Through Repetition

Imagine reading as the art of weaving a vast, intricate tapestry. Each book acts like a pass of the shuttle, adding new threads that enhance the pattern, deepen the color, or reinforce the structure of the weave. Even when the colors seem familiar, perhaps bland, every thread contributes to the strength and beauty of the final product. This analogy perfectly captures the value of repetitive engagement with similar themes across various literary works. It's not merely about encountering new ideas; it's about reinforcing and deepening our understanding of those we've met before, adding layers to our intellectual and emotional fabric. Kemi Nekvapil's The Gift of Asking serves as a brilliant example of such reinforcement in my personal reading journey.

Nekvapil's book, primarily aimed at empowering women to assert their needs without guilt, at first glance might not resonate with everyone, notably someone like myself: a white man far removed from the intersectional feminist perspectives that the book champions. However, its core message about the importance of asking for what you need reiterates a universal theme found in many other self-help and empowerment texts. Each book on this theme that I have encountered has been like another pass of the weaver's shuttle, each adding a slightly different hue to the pattern, influenced by the unique background and perspective of its author.

Reading The Gift of Asking might have felt like covering familiar ground, as it echoes many of the principles I've seen in other works: the significance of recognising one's worth, the power in vulnerability, and the courage required to articulate one's needs. Yet, it is exactly this repetition. Seeing these ideas expressed again, but through Nekvapil's specific lens, that has reinforced these concepts for me. Each repetition adds a background layer to the weave, a subtly varied texture only noticed on repeat viewings. With each pass, the message sinks deeper, the nuance more pronounced.

The repetition serves another crucial purpose: it builds resilience in belief. Just as a tapestry needs multiple threads to become strong enough to withstand wear, our convictions require repeated exposure to ideas to become robust enough to stand up to life's challenges. Encountering the same themes across different contexts also enhances our ability to apply these ideas in various aspects of our own lives, much like how a tapestry's pattern becomes more discernible the more threads are added.

This repetitive reading has also fostered a deeper empathy and understanding within me. While The Gift of Asking might articulate experiences and challenges that are not directly my own, each reading of similar themes across different demographics broadens my perspective. It allows me to see the world through others' eyes more clearly, adding to the richness and diversity of my intellectual tapestry.

The beauty of this weave lies not just in its aesthetic or strength but in its capacity to reflect growth. Each book read and re-read, each theme revisited, does not merely pass by unnoticed. It leaves a mark, alters a view, or strengthens an understanding. As my tapestry grows with each book, so too does my appreciation for the varied and sometimes repetitive threads that compose it. Books like The Gift of Asking do not need to shatter the earth with novelty; their power lies in their ability to reinforce and deepen our understanding of vital truths about human nature and personal growth. Each pass of the shuttle, each repetitive reading, enriches, making it more beautiful, more nuanced, and stronger.

2

The Bittersweet Symphony of Artistic Persistence

I've been thinking a lot about what it takes to keep going as an artist when no one's really watching. Or worse, when they're watching, and still not clapping. That's been on my mind after rewatching Tick, Tick... Boom! and stumbling across the line in Hobo Johnson's song Happiness:

"It's going to take like 4, 5 books no one would ever like for you to live that wonderful life."

And man, if that didn't hit me right in the spleen. That weird little fleshy place where hope and anxiety hang out and whisper insecurities to each other. Because that? That line is the grind.

Watching Tick, Tick... Boom! was like watching someone else live inside my head. Jonathan Larson is turning 30, trying to write the next great American musical, and feeling like time's running out. I'm not a composer, but I've sat in that exact emotional folding chair. The one where you're balancing ambition on one knee and self-doubt on the other, and every time you shift your weight, something creaks.

I saw myself in his obsession. That desperate need to make something good before the clock runs out, even if no one else is asking for it. That constant negotiation with yourself: Why do I do this? Am I still allowed to call myself an artist if nothing I make really "lands"?

It's not dramatic; it's just reality. You pour everything into something and sometimes the return is silence. Or worse. Polite silence.

That lyric from Happiness stuck in my head like gum on a boot. "It's going to take like 4, 5 books no one would ever like…"—yeah, okay, thanks, that's exactly what I needed to hear, Hobo. Except, weirdly, it was. Because there's something oddly comforting about hearing it put so plainly. Not romanticised. Not "follow your dreams and everything will work out." Just: This is going to suck for a while. Probably a long while. And maybe always.

That lyric makes me think about all the work I've already done that didn't go anywhere. The drafts that never saw daylight. The projects I was excited about until I reread them and wanted to climb into a hole lined with rejection slips and irony. But here's the thing: I don't regret making any of it.

Well, maybe a couple pieces. But for the most part, each one taught me something. Even if it was just that I needed to edit more, or sleep occasionally, or stop trying to write essays after eating a full pizza. The point is, I've learned to embrace the failures. I mean, not like them—but acknowledge them as part of the terrain. Like potholes on a road you're committed to driving down barefoot.

No one's out there begging me to keep writing. There's no gallery waiting. No publishers banging down my door. And yet, here I am. Typing. Thinking. Creating. Because I don't know how not to. Because sometimes, writing something helps me feel real. Even if the thing I make only resonates with me, that's still something. It's a quiet kind of persistence. Not glamorous. Just me, hunched over a keyboard, trying to get a sentence to not suck. There's no montage music playing in the background. Just the occasional sound of me groaning at a bad metaphor and trying again.

Every now and then, I wonder how long I'll do this. How long I'll keep showing up to the blank page with my little cup of lukewarm optimism. I don't have a real answer. But I do know this: I've made peace with the idea that I might be one of those people who writes 4, 5 things no one will ever like. And maybe that makes it a wonderful life.

What matters is that I keep showing up. That I keep chasing something I believe in, even if it never becomes anything more than a drawer full of almosts. Because honestly? Some days, creating anything feels like a little rebellion against the idea that everything needs to be perfect, or popular, or profitable.

Sometimes, it's enough just to say: I made this. It exists. I exist.

3

Polysecure Taught Me to Love Louder and Ask Softer

Every once in a while, a book comes along that feels less like reading and more like being gently whacked upside the head with a velvet-covered truth brick. For me, Polysecure by Jessica Fern was exactly that. It didn't just describe my attachment style, it practically handed me a mirror, a megaphone, and a therapy dog all at once. And not in the usual, "oh, interesting psychological insight" way. No, this was more like finding the missing instruction manual for my entire emotional operating system.

First revelation: attachment theory isn't just about clingy toddlers and helicopter parents. Fern reframed attachment in a way that spoke to adult relationships, not just the monogamous ones we're all supposed to build our lives around like Lego castles either. Suddenly, attachment wasn't something that existed in a tight, anxious little 1:1 romantic box. It was everywhere: in friendships, family, communities. It wasn't just "How do I get a boyfriend?" It was "How do I feel secure across all the relationships that actually matter to me?"

Cue the second revelation, even bigger: I don't want just partners. I want deep, intimate, reliant attachments with the people already around me.

Relationships that aren't sexual, aren't romantic, but are textured and important. Friendships with extra gravity. Like the Moon to the Earth, not the Moon to a random passing comet.

Looking back, I realise I've been chasing that kind of connection for a while without having the words for it. Those moments where I felt closest to someone, but things got weird because we didn't have a neat social label for it. Without realising it, I kept folding deep friendship and emotional reliance into a dating framework (because that's the only way our culture teaches us to make people matter).

Polysecure blew that assumption to smithereens and handed me something way better: permission. Permission to just ask for the specific closeness I want without loading it with all the baggage of romantic expectations, without silently hoping people will mind-read me into security.

Want to hold someone's hand? Ask. Want someone to show up for you at a life event? Ask. Want more physical intimacy that isn't sexual? Ask.

Not in a desperate, clingy way. Not in a transactional, "if you don't say yes, I'll collapse" way. Just clear, respectful, open-hearted asking.

And it's not just about getting my needs met. It's about letting other people be their full selves, too. When you strip away the assumptions, when you don't treat a "yes" as the start of a thousand unspoken contracts everything gets lighter, more honest. Rejection isn't a death sentence. Acceptance isn't a life sentence. It's just a moment of real connection, whether the answer is yes or no.

This shift has already started changing the way I move through life. I see certain relationships where I feel vulnerable, personal, close – and now I know: these are the ones I want to nurture. Not by defaulting into romance, not by pretending those feelings don't exist, but by weaving our lives together more deliberately. By asking for more where it feels good to do so.

Yeah, sure, sometimes my brain wants to throw a little fit about whether it's "predatory" to want deeper attachment. Old scripts die hard. But honestly, everyone needs support. Everyone needs their people. And offering connection, while respecting boundaries, is not a crime. It's actually how the entire human species survived long enough to invent things like s'mores and TikTok dances.

So here's the simple, messy, revolutionary practice I'm building: Name the need. Make the ask. Hold it lightly. Try again.

If Polysecure gave me anything, it's the understanding that secure attachment isn't about clutching tighter. It's about building strong bridges. Bridges you can walk across freely, whether it's a quiet Tuesday or a total life meltdown.

And honestly? I want a life full of those bridges. Full of hand-holding, spooning, showing-up-for-each-other, ridiculous levels of non-romantic intimacy. Full of relationships that aren't defined by sex or dating apps or Hallmark cards, but by the simple fact that we chose each other, over and over, in small and big ways.

And the best part? All I have to do is ask.

4

Cuddles, Chaos, and Consent: New Rules for Intimacy

There's something disorienting about realising the way you've been doing relationships your entire life has never really fit you. Like using a pillow moulded to someone else's face. That's where I was for almost a decade. I stepped into friendships like they were lifeboats, hoping for intimacy, and ended up capsizing them with unspoken assumptions. I stepped into monogamous relationships with a kind of half-honesty, squeezing parts of myself into corners, trying not to inconvenience the *Other* with my inconvenient needs. And all the while, I had this vague sense that I could find a way to make it work, with the right combination of friends, family and partners.

Then I read The Art of Relationship Anarchy by Deanne Meyers. Or, more accurately, I devoured it in one sitting. Like it was a survival manual and I'd been stranded on a desert island of mismatched expectations and awkward breakups for the past decade. Every page felt like someone had cracked open my ribcage, peeked at my tangled relationship history, and said, "Oh, honey, no wonder."

Meyers didn't just present a new model. She handed me the missing vocabulary for experiences I'd been stumbling through blindly: the half-asked connections, the moments of intimacy outside traditional boxes, the deep friendships that buckled under the weight of misaligned expectations. Relationship Anarchy (RA) felt like a lifeline.

What got me wasn't just the rejection of monogamous norms (though, yeah, those had been tripping me up since forever). It was the radical idea that a relationship could be whatever two (or more) people wanted it to be. That you could ask for emotional closeness without the default settings of exclusivity, ownership, or long-term coupledom. That you could want to hold someone's hand at a concert without that gesture dragging a whole U-Haul of implications behind it.

I used to think I had two options: ask someone out and get locked into the traditional script, or say nothing and stay on the sidelines of my own emotional life. Spoiler: neither worked. I lost friendships by trying to make them into something they weren't, and I wrecked romantic relationships by trying to make them into something *I* wasn't. I didn't want the full buffet of expectations, just a slice. Maybe some physical closeness. Maybe a recurring weekly hangout. Maybe shared community or emotional intimacy. But because I didn't know how to ask for that without triggering the whole monogamy script, I fumbled, hard.

One of the worst ones was with a friend. We had built this quiet closeness, spent weekends together, shared secrets, leaned on each other when life was heavy. And then one night, I asked them out. Not because I wanted a capital-R Relationship, but because I didn't know how else to validate the depth of what we had. It wrecked everything. They felt blindsided, betrayed even. The intimacy we had just collapsed under the weight of mismatched assumptions. I lost one of the most important people in my life because I didn't know that there was a third path. That we could have shaped our connection in a way that honored what it was, without trying to squeeze it into the wrong box.

Now? I just ask.

I ask to cuddle during movies. I ask to dance, to hold hands, to share weekly routines, to meet family. Not because I want to put someone on a relationship pedestal, but because those are the ways I connect. I ask like a person who knows what they need and trusts the other person to know what they can give. That's the engine of RA: consent and communication. Clear, ongoing, slightly-scary honesty that lets relationships become what they are, not what they're *'supposed'* to be.

RA refuses the idea that love and connection need to be ranked or contained at all. It says you can love ten people, in ten different ways, and not one of them needs to be prioritised just because it involves sex, or cohabitation, or shared bank accounts. It says friendship can be as sacred as romance. It says you can design your relationships like a playlist, not an album. Pick the tracks that move you, skip the ones that don't.

This way of living relationships lets things be fluid. It means a friend can become a sexual partner and back again, without a meltdown. It means a romantic connection can scale up or down, shift shape, turn sideways. You can co-parent with one person, build a creative partnership with another, and have regular cuddles with a third, all without the pyramid scheme of emotional hierarchy. The connections don't have to compete. They just have to fit, with everyone consensually buying in.

And yeah, it's risky.

RA doesn't come with guardrails. You can screw up the communication. You can get it wrong. You can hurt people if you're not careful, or if you're not honest with yourself. You can say, "I'm fine with this" when you're not. You can lie to yourself about what you want. But I've blown up relationships under monogamous norms too. At least now, when I take risks, they feel like they're leading somewhere closer to home. Not perfect, but honest. Not simple, but aligned.

This isn't a dating strategy. It's an approach to connection and intimacy. It means valuing community, showing up for chosen family, being brave enough to ask for what I want without trying to own it. It means trusting people to say yes or no without the world ending. It means letting go of the fantasy of The One and leaning into the beautiful chaos of the many. It's still messy, but at least it's *my* mess, built with intention, consent, and a little bit of dance-floor hand-holding.

And honestly, that's a revolution I can live with.

5

bell hooks Said It Better: Her Feminism Is a Welcome Mat, Not a Lecture

Most people hear the word feminism and immediately brace for impact. Somewhere between sensational headlines, Twitter brawls, and that one uncle who only brings up "misandry" at Thanksgiving, feminism got a PR problem. It's often presented like a courtroom drama where men are on trial and women are divided into victims and angry prosecutors. Enter bell hooks. With a book in one hand, and intellectual machete in the other, ready to hack through all that noise with Feminism is for Everybody.

And she does it with no yelling, no shaming, and definitely no finger-pointing. Just devastating clarity and one of the most inclusive, disarming uses of language I've ever seen. The brilliance of Hooks isn't just in what she says, it's in how she says it. Her control of ideas and language is like watching someone juggle chainsaws while gently explaining patriarchy to a room full of skeptics. Nobody gets hurt, and somehow everyone leaves feeling more human.

She Doesn't Blame

Hooks doesn't build her argument by blaming men or exalting women. Instead, she writes about systems (patriarchy, domination, capitalism) and how they seep into every corner of our lives like a broken faucet dripping poison. Her framing is surgical. Rather than say men do this to women, she says patriarchy trains us all to dominate or be dominated. Feminist isn't about swapping who's on top. It's about dismantling the whole hierarchy.

That shift in framing is everything. Because now, the conversation isn't about you vs. them. It's about all of us vs. this system. The system that's wrecking us all. And that's a wildly different invitation. Instead of creating enemies, it creates space for accountability. You feel seen, not scolded. Responsible, not attacked.

Everyone's in the Frame

Hooks pulls off the rare trick of making everyone both the victim and the culprit. You see how you've been hurt, but also how you're also holding the knife. That duality is what makes this book so transformative. It doesn't excuse behavior, it connects it to the system that taught us all the wrong dance moves from birth.

And she doesn't just do this with men, it's the system in which everyone partakes. She calls out women, how women uphold sexism, how women dominate each other, how internalised patriarchy makes us all perform roles we didn't audition for. But she does it without smugness. There's no intellectual gotcha here. Just a calm, clear-eyed truth.

Language That Liberates

Hooks' language is so accessible, so stripped of ego and academic puffery, that it bypasses defensiveness. You don't feel like you're reading a lecture. You feel like you're having a deeply necessary conversation with someone who actually wants to understand you, and wants you to understand yourself.

She avoids the buzzwords that get people's hackles up. I've said patriarchy more in this article than she does in the entire book. No overreliance on niche theory terms. No "if you don't get it, you're part of the problem" posturing. Instead, she writes like a teacher who actually wants her students to learn, not just clap for how smart she is. And that tone, pwohh... Measured, open, curious. It allows the ideas to land with people who might normally tune out anything wrapped in the word feminist.

Framing Feminism

The mainstream caricature of feminism, man-blaming, woman-worshipping echo chamber, could not be further from Hooks' vision. That's part of the tragedy. When feminism becomes clickbait, it loses its heart. It becomes reactive and blaming instead of transformative.

Hooks sidesteps all of that by refusing to play the blame game. Instead, she plays the long game. She invites readers to reimagine a world that doesn't revolve around domination. And she does it without compromising. Her ideas are radical, but her delivery is warm. The result? A book that doesn't scream for attention, but changes you and pushes for an equal, just world.

Hooks doesn't organise her thinking around identity groups. She organises it around domination. Gender-based domination. Racial domination. Class domination. Sexual domination. She doesn't list out every demographic and plead their case one by one. She doesn't have to. Her framing is so expansive, it folds everyone in automatically.

Because who hasn't felt crushed by some system or authority? Who hasn't feared being overpowered, unseen, or controlled? In that way, Feminism is for Everybody becomes a kind of spiritual chiropractic adjustment. It realigns your sense of justice and makes it obvious that feminism, real feminism, (the radical kind that Hooks preaches) isn't about revenge. It's about release.

Feminism is for Everybody is a masterclass in linguistic strategy, emotional intelligence, and radical empathy. Hooks shows how you can tell the truth, the whole ugly systemic truth, without turning readers into villains or victims. It's feminism that disarms, not because it waters things down, but because it knows the difference between burning bridges and lighting the way.

So, if you've ever felt left out of the gender conversation, or like feminism was something happening over there without you. This is the book! It isn't about making you feel good. It's about making you feel seen, implicated, and ready to do something. It shows exactly what the title states, feminism is for everyone.

6

The Absurdity of Extremes: Middleground in Heartbreak High

In the labyrinth of modern television, few shows have dared to tread the tightrope of political discourse with the audacity of "Heartbreak High." The second season delves into the tumultuous waters of hyper-liberalism and hyper-conservatism, presenting a tableau of characters who embody the extremes of these ideologies. At the heart of this narrative is Queeny, a character whose personal relationships serve as a microcosm for the societal schisms that plague our increasingly polarised world.

Queeny's interactions with her peers are devoid of the political jargon that often muddies the waters of discourse. Instead, she engages with them on a level that is profoundly human, eschewing labels and preconceived notions to be unequivocally herself. Her approach is a refreshing antidote to the absurdity of extremes that dominate swaths of modern media and other online spaces, where individuals are often reduced to caricatures of their beliefs.

The series paints a vivid picture of the pitfalls of hyper-liberalism, where the pursuit of progressiveness can sometimes devolve into a performative contest. Characters who espouse these views are depicted as well-meaning but ultimately misguided, their actions driven more by a desire for social validation than genuine conviction. In the real world, we see instances of hyper-liberalism in various social media campaigns that, while well-intentioned, may focus more on the number of shares and likes than on meaningful engagement with the issues at hand.

The pursuit of a particular liberal ideal can sometimes lead to a homogenisation of thought, where differing opinions are not just unwelcome but actively suppressed. This is particularly evident in the phenomenon of cancel culture, which often punishes individuals for past mistakes without allowing space for growth or redemption. The absurdity of these extremes becomes apparent when the quest for progressiveness overlooks the importance of dialogue and understanding. True social change requires patience, empathy, and the inclusion of a wide range of viewpoints, something Heartbreak High's liberal characters often lack.

Moving away from the polarising rhetoric of hyper-liberalism, we can foster a more inclusive society that values both individual freedoms and collective responsibility. In essence, while hyper-liberalism seeks to champion progressive values, it must be wary of becoming the very force it opposes by marginalising those who think differently. A balanced approach that encourages open dialogue and respects diverse perspectives is essential for a healthy, functioning society. It's about finding the middle ground where progress can be made without sacrificing the richness of human experience and the diversity of thought that drives innovation and understanding.

Conversely, "Heartbreak High" also casts a critical eye on hyper-conservatism, portraying it as a bastion of rigidity and resistance to change. Characters who cling to conservative values are shown to be fearful of the unknown, their worldview constrained by the boundaries of tradition. Hyper-conservatism manifests in various ways: the reluctance to accept new social norms or technologies, leading to a romanticisation of the past and a demonisation of the future. This fear of the unknown can create echo chambers, especially on social media platforms, where like-minded individuals reinforce each other's beliefs without exposure to alternative viewpoints.

The result is a feedback loop that not only reinforces insularity but also contributes to the polarisation of society. As these echo chambers grow stronger, the middle ground becomes increasingly narrow, making it difficult for people to engage in constructive dialogue. The divide between 'us' and 'them' widens, and the ability to empathise with those who hold different views diminishes. This phenomenon is not limited to any one platform or medium; it is a reflection of the human tendency to seek out confirmation of our pre-existing beliefs. However, the algorithms that govern social media platforms like TikTok often exacerbate this tendency by curating content that aligns with our interests and views, further entrenching us in our ideological silos.

To overcome the pitfalls of hyper-conservatism, it's essential to foster environments that encourage open-mindedness and a willingness to engage with new ideas. It requires a conscious effort to step outside of our comfort zones and consider perspectives that challenge our assumptions. Only by doing so can we hope to bridge the divides that separate us and work towards a more inclusive and dynamic society. In essence, while hyper-conservatism seeks to preserve valuable traditions, it must also allow for adaptation and growth. Balancing respect for the past with openness to the future is key to navigating the complexities of the modern world. It's about finding harmony between the tried-and-true and the new-and-possible, creating a society that honors its roots while reaching for the stars.

Queeny's relationships offer a blueprint for navigating these treacherous ideological waters. Her ability to connect with others on a personal level, to see beyond the veneer of their political affiliations, is a testament to the power of empathy. She recognises that the mess society finds itself in cannot be tidied up with broad strokes of liberalism or conservatism. Instead, it requires a nuanced understanding of the individual stories that make up our collective experience.

The show's portrayal of Queeny's world is a mirror held up to our own, reflecting the absurdity of the extremes that have come to define our online and offline interactions. It challenges viewers to consider the impact of their words and actions, to question the narratives they subscribe to, and to seek common ground in the shared humanity that binds us all. "Heartbreak High" is a cultural touchstone that captures the zeitgeist of our times. Through Queeny's journey, it offers a poignant critique of the extremes that threaten to tear the fabric of society apart. It is a call to action, urging us to embrace the complexity of our world and to find solace in the simple, yet profound, connections that unite us.

7

When Identity Becomes Everything: Finding Balance Again

Reading The Madness of Crowds by Douglas Murray feels a bit like being offered a conspiracy theory. But one where you awkwardly realise... he might be onto something. At its core, Murray's biggest warning is simple: we've turned identity into a competitive sport, and everyone's too busy measuring their marginalisation points to notice the house burning down around them.

And he's right.

There was a time when identity politics was about finding solidarity. Queer folks found community. Women fought for rights that actually changed lives. Racial minorities pushed forward societal progress that mattered: voting rights, anti-discrimination laws, basic decency. But somewhere along the way, the good-faith fight metastasised into a weird, exhausting tournament. Now, it feels like everyone's got a player card: race, gender, sexuality, neurotype (bonus points if you can throw in a complicated relationship with capitalism).

Instead of building bridges, identity became a tax form: complicated, tedious, and designed to separate you into as many tiny categories as possible. As if humanity was just a collection of checkboxes instead of messy, glorious contradictions. You aren't just a person anymore; you're a brand.

This is where Murray's book shines, and also where it starts to sag under its own weight. He makes sharp observations about how these endless splinterings of identity actually weaken the very solidarity they were meant to foster. But then he ruins the moment by cherry-picking the most absurd examples he can find, the intellectual equivalent of holding up a clown and saying, "See? The whole circus is silly." It feels less like an invitation to think, and more like being badgered into agreement. And if you're someone who values critical thinking, the "trust me, it's all this bad" tone sets off more alarms than a hotel fire drill.

Because identity isn't the enemy. There are beautiful, new frontiers being explored in gender, race, and sexuality. New ways of understanding each other that should be celebrated. But when we turn every aspect of who we are into an exclusive club, a point system, or worse, a grievance Olympics, we lose the thread entirely. We forget the real enemy isn't who gets to sit at which table, but the fact that the whole damn dining hall is falling apart.

And while Murray sidesteps it (probably because of his own political views and backers) the most damning effect of identity games is this. They distract us from the fights that actually matter. Economic inequality. The climate crisis. Healthcare access. The stuff that crushes everyone, marginalised or not. Instead, we burn endless energy arguing over whether someone with three marginalised identities is automatically more right than someone with two, while billionaires buy elections and the planet quietly melts.

At the end of the day, The Madness of Crowds isn't perfect. Not by a long shot. But it does crack open a hard truth: if we don't start treating identity as part of who we are instead of the whole story, we'll keep splintering until there's no "we" left.

8

Monsters in Thought or Action: Comparing Nightcrawler & American Psycho

At a glance, Nightcrawler (2014) and American Psycho (2000) seem to tell a similar story. Men detached from morality, chasing success in a world that barely notices the damage they leave behind. Both films offer unsettling portraits of masculinity, ambition, and power, showing characters who perform their roles in society flawlessly while concealing something terrifying beneath the surface.

Despite their similarities, they leave the audience with entirely different conclusions. They don't just differ in tone, one unsettlingly funny, the other uncomfortably real, but in what they ask us to take away. American Psycho plays with the idea of monstrous thoughts and suggests that what truly matters is action. Nightcrawler moves in the opposite direction, it shows that in a world that rewards ruthless ambition, only results matter.

One film makes you laugh at the absurdity of a broken system. The other forces you to realise that, within that system, the worst people thrive.

A Different Kind of Uncomfortable
Watching American Psycho feels like sitting next to a lunatic on a train and

realising he's too busy talking about The Matrix to actually be dangerous. Watching Nightcrawler feels like not noticing the guy next to you; but, if a shooter appears, he'll use you as a human shield and then not call an ambulance.

The humor in American Psycho is immediate. Patrick Bateman, played with eerie precision by Christian Bale, is an absurd character. His morning routine, his obsession with status, his desperate need to be perceived as better than those around him. It's all so exaggerated to the point of comedic satire. His violence, too, is ridiculous. He stages his murders like they're theatrical performances, blaring pop music while hacking people to pieces. The film's satirical tone makes it clear: Bateman is a hollow man in a hollow world, and that world is so self-absorbed that even a serial killer barely registers.

Nightcrawler offers no such release. Lou Bloom, played by Jake Gyllenhaal, doesn't have any of Bateman's obvious red flags. He isn't a caricature. He isn't a parody. He's something worse, believable. He's polite, soft-spoken, and always professional. He uses business jargon and self-help rhetoric to justify his every move. Unlike Bateman, whose violent fantasies may not even be real, Lou's darkness isn't theoretical. He acts on it, over and over again, and the world not only lets him but encourages him.

Bateman is an exaggerated joke. Lou is a reflection of reality, and that's why he lingered under my skin for days afterwards.

Thoughts vs. Actions

At the heart of both films is a question. What matters more: what someone thinks and believes, or what they do?

American Psycho leans into this question with its ambiguous ending. If Bateman never actually killed anyone, what does that mean? Is he still a monster, or just a man with violent fantasies? The film suggests that in a world as superficial as his, it doesn't matter. No one would care either way. But if we take the ending at face value, it presents an idea that's oddly reassuring: no matter how dark someone's thoughts may be, it's their actions that define them. Bateman, for all his psychosis, is ultimately powerless. He wants to kill, but his world is so detached from reality that even murder doesn't register. He remains stuck in his own loop, fantasising about control but never truly taking it.

Lou, on the other hand, takes power, swinging it like a sociopathic scalpel. He isn't interested in thoughts or impulses. He doesn't waste time on rage or ego. He just acts, and because he never hesitates, he succeeds. This is what makes Nightcrawler so disturbing. Lou's thoughts don't matter. The system rewards him for what he does, and what he does is learn, adapt, and manipulate.

In American Psycho, Bateman's thoughts are horrific, but they ultimately don't shape his reality. His actions are neutral, Bateman's an arse, but he doesn't kill anyone. In Nightcrawler, Lou's thoughts might be neutral, he isn't inherently cruel or violent, but in the system he exists a lack of morality allows him to rise. Bateman is trapped in his own mind. Lou responds to the incentives around him, regardless of moral consequence.

The Horror of Success

Both films deal with ambition, but they present success in drastically different ways. American Psycho is about a man who should have everything but ultimately has nothing. Bateman's story is one of stagnation, his final monologue even admits as much. He isn't punished, but he also isn't rewarded. He just exists, continuing his meaningless cycle in a world that has already forgotten him.

Nightcrawler, by contrast, is about a man who starts with nothing and wins. The horror isn't that Lou is caught, it's that he's rewarded. By the end, he has a thriving business, employees, and the ability to shape the very media landscape he once merely filmed. Unlike Bateman, he doesn't just remain in his loop.

And this is where the films leave us with two drastically different take-aways.American Psycho reassures us, in a twisted way. It suggests that Bateman, a monster on the inside, is restrained by a system that responds to actions not thoughts. This renders his horrific fantasies terrifying but mute. Nightcrawler, on the other hand, offers no such comfort. Lou wins because of action, depraved action that gets him ahead. It's rigged in favor of people like him, who have no internal barometer for their actions.

Bateman is terrifying because of what he wants to do. Lou is terrifying because of what he does. And in the world we live in, that second kind of monster is the one that is truly terrifying.

The Monsters We Accept

Both Nightcrawler and American Psycho ask the same question: What kind of darkness can we live with? What kind of monster is easier to tolerate? And for me, the answer is simple. I can handle a Bateman. I can't handle a Lou.

Bateman is repulsive, sure, but he's ridiculous. He's an over-the-top, self-obsessed mess of a man who is trapped inside his own head. He has all these horrifying, intrusive thoughts, but what does he actually do? A man with dangerous thoughts but no real impact on the world is just another broken person who needs help.

Lou, though? Lou is a different kind of nightmare. He isn't weighed down by inner turmoil. He isn't driven by deep-seated rage or psychosis. He isn't fantasising about control, he's out there taking it. And he's able to do it because he understands something crucial about the world: people don't care what you think, only what you do. Lou doesn't have violent impulses, but he's more dangerous than Bateman because he has no hesitation. He sees opportunities where others see ethical lines, and he crosses them without flinching.

That's the real horror of Nightcrawler. Lou isn't a traditional villain. He isn't some raging, murderous psychopath. He's just efficient. He's a product of a system that rewards ambition, no matter how detached from morality it is. The film doesn't end with him getting caught. It doesn't punish him. It hands him the keys to his own company and tells him to go forth and conquer. It's not a story about a man descending into madness. It's a story about a man succeeding because he never had any moral baggage to slow him down in the first place.

I'd rather be in a room with Bateman than Lou. Bateman might want to kill me, but he's too wrapped up in his own performance of being Patrick Bateman to actually go through with it. Lou wouldn't want to kill me, but if my death got him a better filming angle, he'd step right over my body to get the footage.

One film presents a monster trapped by his own fantasies. The other presents a monster created and rewarded by the world around him.

That's what makes Nightcrawler so much harder to shake.

9

Interpreting Masculinity: Character Analysis of 'The Hitman's Bodyguard'

"The Hitman's Bodyguard," a 2017 action-comedy film directed by Patrick Hughes, offers an engaging exploration of two contrasting masculine characters: Michael Bryce (Ryan Reynolds), a meticulous and detail-oriented professional bodyguard, and Darius Kincaid (Samuel L. Jackson), an audacious and spontaneous hitman. By juxtaposing these two characters' disparate approaches to masculinity, the film provides a critique of the societal norms and expectations of masculinity and prompts a broader discourse on the meaning and expression of masculinity in contemporary society.

Michael Bryce embodies a type of masculinity rooted in control, precision, and professional success. He meticulously plans his every move and favors a rigid, organised lifestyle over spontaneity or recklessness. His masculine identity hinges heavily on his professional reputation, thus underlining societal expectations of men as providers and achievers. However, this strict adherence to order and perfection is shown to be a double-edged sword. When Bryce loses a client, his professional reputation crumbles, causing him to question his worth and capabilities – a depiction that underscores the pressures and insecurities men often face in a society that equates masculinity with success and control.

Contrastingly, Darius Kincaid embodies a different form of masculinity, one that thrives on audacity, spontaneity, and rugged charm. His aggressive style, fearless demeanor, and cavalier approach to life represent a hyper-masculine archetype that, while often glorified, can also be destructive and unsustainable. The film employs Kincaid's character to illustrate how extreme forms of masculinity can lead to conflict, recklessness, and an unstable lifestyle. However, Kincaid's character also provides a critique of the societal stigma associated with male emotional expression. Unlike Bryce, Kincaid openly expresses his feelings, especially his love for his wife Sonia (Salma Hayek). He's not afraid to show his vulnerabilities, challenging the societal stereotype that men must always be stoic and emotionally resilient.

The relationship between Bryce and Kincaid forms the crux of the film, providing a platform for the exploration and eventual reconciliation of their contrasting masculinities. They bicker, argue, and constantly challenge each other's approach to masculinity, reflecting the wider societal discourse on the evolving definitions of masculinity. Their journey from mutual disdain to grudging respect and eventual friendship highlights the notion that there's no singular way to be masculine; instead, masculinity can encompass a spectrum of behaviors, attitudes, and values.

"The Hitman's Bodyguard" uses humor and action to shed light on the societal expectations of masculinity and the pressure these expectations can exert on men. It shows that extreme forms of masculinity, whether it's an obsessive focus on control and professional success or reckless audacity and aggressiveness, can be damaging and restrictive.

"The Hitman's Bodyguard" presents a compelling critique of traditional masculinity norms through its portrayal of two contrasting characters, Michael Bryce and Darius Kincaid. It underscores the need for society to embrace a more nuanced understanding of masculinity. One that values emotional expressiveness, personal growth, and mutual respect. By doing so, the film invites viewers to engage in a broader dialogue about the meaning of masculinity and the importance of allowing men to define their own identities outside societal norms.

10

The Paradox of Influence: Navigating the Crossroads of Power and Empathy

The books "How to Win Friends and Influence People" by Dale Carnegie and "How to Make People Like You in 90 Seconds or Less" by Nicholas Boothman have titles that immediately grab attention. They promise swift mastery in the arts of persuasion and likability, skills traditionally associated with acquiring money and power. Yet, paradoxically, the core messages within these books advocate for authenticity, empathy, and genuine human connection. This essay explores the contrast between the appeal of the titles for individuals seeking wealth and influence and the deeper, more altruistic principles these books promote.

The titles of these books are undeniably appealing to those who equate success with money and power. In a capitalist society, where personal advancement is often measured in such terms, the ability to influence others and quickly make friends is seen as a fast track to success. "How to Win Friends and Influence People" suggests a formulaic approach to winning over others, which, on the surface, seems like a tool for manipulation towards one's own ends. Similarly, "How to Make People Like You in 90 Seconds or Less" implies a quick-fix strategy to a complex human challenge. In doing so these books appeal to those who desire immediate results in social settings.

However, once the covers are cracked open, readers find that the content of these books is not about manipulation or superficial charm. Instead, both Carnegie and Boothman emphasise the importance of authenticity, empathy, and genuine interest in others. Carnegie's book, for instance, doesn't offer tricks to deceive people into being friends or allies but rather guides readers on how to cultivate qualities like empathy, active listening, and appreciation for others' perspectives. His principles encourage a deeper understanding of human nature and promote respect and kindness as the foundations for any relationship.

Similarly, Boothman's book, while promising a quick connection, delves into the art of effective communication, emphasising the importance of body language, attentiveness, and the ability to genuinely relate to others. The '90 seconds' is not a gimmick to fool others into liking someone but an encouragement to make the most of the initial moments of interaction by being authentically present and open.

The appeal of these titles, therefore, lies in a cultural paradox. On one hand, there's an almost universal desire for quick success, influence, and the ability to navigate social situations to one's advantage: goals often associated with a hunger for money and power. On the other hand, there's a deep-seated human need for genuine connection, understanding, and mutual respect: values that are fundamentally altruistic and empathetic. These books cater to both impulses. They draw readers in with the promise of social mastery; but, then guide them towards principles of sincerity and personal integrity.

This dichotomy reflects broader societal tensions between individual ambition and communal well-being. The titles speak to individualistic aspirations, yet the content advocates for a more collectivist approach to relationships. In doing so, these books inadvertently highlight the potential for reconciliation between these seemingly conflicting desires. They suggest that success, influence, and likability are not merely tools for personal gain but can be achieved through genuine, empathetic engagement with others.

"How to Win Friends and Influence People" and "How to Make People Like You in 90 Seconds or Less" serve as intriguing case studies in the appeal of personal advancement contrasted with the virtues of authentic human connection. Their titles might attract those seeking a quick path to money and power, but their content redirects readers to the more fulfilling and ultimately more sustainable path of empathy, respect, and genuine interaction. In a world often torn between individual success and collective well-being, these books offer a bridge, suggesting that the two are not mutually exclusive but are, in fact, deeply interconnected.

11

Authenticity vs. Performance in Relationship Building: A Dive into Dale Carnegie's Legacy

In the realm of face-to-face relationship building, Dale Carnegie's "How to Win Friends and Influence People" stands as the quintessential guidebook. It's akin to the holy grail in a world thirsty for connection and influence. Yet, as we peel back the layers of Carnegie's advice, we're met with a conundrum that's as perplexing as choosing the right emoji in a high-stakes text conversation: the battle between authenticity and performance.

At first glance, following Carnegie's principles might seem like slapping on a metaphorical neon sign that screams, "I'm friendly, trust me!", a beacon of desperation in the social seas. This perspective views his advice as a performance, a series of strategic moves on the chessboard of social interaction. It's like deciding to wear a superhero costume to a job interview: sure, you'll stand out, but will people take you seriously?

But let's not be too hasty in casting Carnegie's insights into the shadows of manipulation. Perhaps, the essence of his teachings isn't about donning a persona or engaging in a well-rehearsed performance. Maybe it's more about refining your natural tendencies to harmonise with the social symphony around you. This isn't about changing the music but learning how to dance to it more gracefully.

Consider the principle of genuine interest in others. On the surface, it might look like you're just ticking off a box in the "how to make friends" checklist. However, when you dive deeper, isn't this what we're all looking for? A sign that someone sees us, hears us, and values us? It's not about pretending to care; it's about unlocking a part of you that genuinely does. Like finding out you actually love broccoli after years of pushing it around your plate, a new undiscovered appreciation.

Then there's the art of remembering names, a Carnegie classic. Sure, you could argue that it's a performance tactic, a way to make someone feel special so they'll like you more. But isn't it also a basic form of respect, an acknowledgment of someone's individuality in a world that often feels too busy to care? It's the difference between receiving a handwritten letter in the mail versus a generic email blast. Both get the message across, but one makes you feel like someone took the time to see you.

This is not to say that the line between authenticity and performance is always clear. Like trying to navigate a foggy road at night, sometimes our intentions get lost in the execution. The key is mindfulness, being aware of why we're applying Carnegie's principles. Are we seeking genuine connection, or are we looking for shortcuts to personal gain? It's the intention that colors our actions, turning them from hollow performances into authentic interactions.

In the dance of face-to-face relationship building, Carnegie's advice serves as both a map and a mirror. It guides us towards more meaningful interactions but also reflects back our intentions. In the end, maybe the question isn't whether we're being authentic or performing. Perhaps it's about whether we're moving towards a world where kindness, respect, and genuine interest are the norm, rather than the exception.

So, as we navigate the delicate balance between authenticity and performance, let's remember that the most powerful connections are built on a foundation of genuine care. It's not about the perfect performance; it's about the perfect imperfections that make each interaction uniquely human. After all, isn't that what Dale Carnegie was trying to teach us all along?

12

Nonviolent Communication and the Choreography of Empathy

Empathy often seems like a mysterious, almost magical human capability, seemingly effortless for some and frustratingly elusive for others. It's like watching a natural dancer glide across a dance floor with innate grace compared to someone who steps hesitantly, counting beats under their breath. However, Marshall Rosenberg's seminal work, *Nonviolent Communication: A Language of Life*, proposes a radical idea: empathy, much like dance, can be choreographed. It can be taught, practiced, and mastered, regardless of one's initial skill level.

The central premise of Rosenberg's Nonviolent Communication (NVC) is that empathy is not just an inborn talent but a learnable, practicable skill. To continue our dance metaphor, if life's emotional exchanges are a dance floor, then NVC is the dance studio where one learns the steps. For those who do not 'hear the music' of emotional cues naturally Rosenberg's structured approach offers a sequence of steps to engage in meaningful, empathetic dialogue.

NVC teaches us to observe without evaluating, to express our feelings and needs, and to make requests rather than demands. These are the basic steps of the empathy dance. For someone like me, who struggles with these aspects of interaction, these steps do not come naturally. We need the music broken down into beats and rhythms that we can follow, a script that tells us when to step forward, when to turn, when to allow space for our partner to move.

Critics might argue that this 'scripted' approach to interaction feels inauthentic, perhaps even manipulative. They might say it's akin to a dancer who only knows a routine by rote and cannot adapt to the changing tempo of the music. Yet, this perspective misses a crucial point: the intent behind the actions.

In dance, whether a dancer improvises or performs a choreographed piece, the aim is to convey emotion and tell a story through movement. The audience does not care if the performance was improvised or meticulously planned; what matters is the authenticity of the emotional expression. Similarly, in communication, if the 'script' of NVC leads to genuine understanding and connection, then the method by which empathy is expressed becomes secondary to the outcome.

Imagine a scenario where an individual who struggles with empathy uses NVC to navigate a difficult conversation with a friend. They use a 'script' to identify their own feelings and express them clearly, "I feel upset because I need more support." They follow the steps of NVC to empathise with their friend and make a clear request without judgment or demand. This structured approach does not diminish the sincerity of the interaction; rather, it facilitates a genuine connection that might not have been possible through spontaneous emotional expression.

Nonviolent Communication, as a choreography of empathy, empowers those of us who find the rhythm of social interaction elusive. It democratises emotional expression, making it accessible to those who need explicit directions on the dance floor of social engagement. Learning to dance, after all, is no less an art for the student who starts with numbered steps on the floor than for the one who seems to sway naturally to the beat.

In the end, the beauty of a dance lies not in the method of its learning but in its performance. Likewise, the value of an empathetic exchange lies not in its spontaneity but in its sincerity and the connection it fosters. Rosenberg's choreographed approach to communication asks us to look beyond the dance steps to appreciate the art of connection they create. A performance that, regardless of how the steps are learned, can be as profound and moving as the most natural dance.

13

Buying Love: Spending and Romance

In the shimmering world of "Pretty Woman," money doesn't just talk; it starts a conversation that can lead to a myriad of relationship dynamics. The film presents us with Vivian and Edward, whose relationship begins with a transaction as clear-cut as a business deal. But as they say, money is a great servant but a terrible master, and this narrative explores the complexities that unfold when wealth becomes the bedrock of a romantic liaison.

Let's start with the basics: a man paying for the first date or showering his interest with lavish gifts. It's a tale as old as time, or at least as old as the concept of dating itself. This gesture, often seen as chivalrous, carries an unspoken expectation of reciprocity. The currency of affection is exchanged for the currency of wealth, and sometimes, this transaction is as straightforward as it gets, a quid pro quo where the lines are drawn, and the boundaries are clear.

Picture this- Jack and Diane, two twenty-somethings decide to take their budding romance to the next level with a dinner date. Jack insists on picking the tab at the swanky new bistro downtown, flashing his cash like he's got a money tree in the backyard. Diane's impressed, sure, but she can't shake the feeling that she now owes him something more than a smile and a thank you.

Fast forward a few weeks, and the pattern's set. Jack's the big spender, showering Diane with gifts that sparkle and shine, each one a silent reminder of the debt she's accruing. It's not long before Diane starts to feel like she's less of a girlfriend and more of an investment, a trophy to be won with the highest bid. The intimacy they once shared, laughing over shared fries at the local diner, is replaced by a transactional chill that no amount of fine dining can warm.

What happens when the stakes are higher, the gifts more opulent, and the expectations grander? Enter "Pretty Woman," where our protagonists' initial relationship is solely based on financial exchange. Edward, a wealthy businessman, hires Vivian, a sex worker, to accompany him to social events. The payment is explicit, the terms are set, and the lifestyle is nothing short of extravagant. It's a hyperbolic portrayal of the dynamic of Jack and Diane.

The benefits of the arrangement glitter like the jewels in a Rodeo Drive boutique. There's clarity and convenience, with both parties understanding the transactional nature of their interaction. It can be empowering, allowing individuals to set their terms and have control over the relationship's trajectory. And sometimes, just sometimes, it can be the catalyst for something deeper, as we see with Vivian and Edward, whose relationship evolves into a genuine connection.

On the smaller stage of everyday relationships, the script isn't written by Hollywood, relationships are messier. When financial gestures are part of the courtship, even in the most mundane of settings, the implications ripple through the waters of intimacy. Take the expectation set when one partner consistently foots the bill for dates or surprises the other with gifts that scream luxury more than sentiment. It's a subtle score that plays in the background, often unheard but always felt, setting a rhythm that can be hard to break.

This rhythm can become a cacophony that drowns out the genuine notes of connection. When one person is always reaching for their wallet, it can create an imbalance that tips the scales of power. It's not just about who pays for dinner; it's about who holds the power to decide where dinner is, the relationship pace, and what the implicit expectations are. The partner without the financial upper hand might feel indebted, obligated to reciprocate in ways that aren't aligned with their true feelings or desires. This dynamic can stifle the growth of any relationship, trapping it in a cycle of expectation and repayment that leaves little room for the organic development of intimacy built on equal footing.

In the end, while "Pretty Woman" wraps up its narrative with a neat, happy bow, the reality is often messier. Relationships built on the bedrock of financial exchange may flourish into something beautiful, but they're just as likely to crumble under the weight of their own artifice. The pursuit of romantic intimacy, when tainted by the expectation of monetary compensation, becomes a hollow endeavor for both men and women. It's a negative trend, one that turns the quest for love into a transaction, and the human heart into a commodity to be bought and sold. As we roll the credits, a reminder, money can buy a lot of things, the depth and authenticity of human connection are not among them.

14

Quirky Hearts: Unconventional Love in 'Eagle vs Shark'

"Eagle vs Shark," directed by Taika Waititi, is a unique exploration of love, relationships, and human connection. This quirky and offbeat film follows the story of two socially awkward individuals, Lily and Jarrod, who find each other through their shared idiosyncrasies and embark on a journey that's both bizarre and heartwarming.

"Eagle vs Shark" depicts love as an acceptance of one's flaws and oddities. Both Lily and Jarrod are not your typical protagonists. They're flawed, eccentric, and often misunderstood by those around them. Lily, with her shy demeanor and quirky habits, and Jarrod, with his grandiose delusions of self-importance, represent the outcasts of society. However, it's through their peculiarities that they connect and understand each other in a way no one else can. This reflects the film's message that love is about finding someone who accepts you for who you are, no matter how strange or unconventional that may be.

The film's narrative doesn't shy away from the awkward and uncomfortable realities of love and relationships. The interactions between Lily and Jarrod are often cringe-worthy, yet they're depicted with a sincerity and honesty that's rare in romantic films. This portrayal challenges the conventional notions of romance, suggesting that love is not always about grand gestures or perfect moments; sometimes, it's about sharing a video game session, dressing up in ridiculous costumes, or simply understanding each other's weirdness.

It explores the theme of personal growth and healing through love. Both characters are dealing with their own emotional baggage and insecurities. As their relationship develops, they confront their past traumas and learn to overcome their fears. This journey is not smooth or idealised; it's messy and real, reflecting the film's belief that love is not just about finding happiness but also about growing and healing together.

"Eagle vs Shark" offers a distinct and unconventional depiction of love. It challenges traditional romantic tropes and presents a story of two peculiar individuals finding solace and understanding in each other's company. The film defines love as an acceptance of one's true self, an embrace of the strange and awkward, and a journey of mutual growth and healing. It's a reminder that love can be found in the most unexpected places and can take the most unexpected forms. Through its unique storytelling and eccentric characters, "Eagle vs Shark" celebrates the odd, the unconventional, and the beautifully imperfect aspects of love.

15

Laughing Through it All: The D&D Energy of Tactical Breach Wizards

Tactical Breach Wizards is great fun. It's a brilliant spin on XCOM-style turn-based combat, but where XCOM has you sweating over every percentage point in a desperate battle for survival, Tactical Breach Wizards lets you punt a riot cop out a fourth-story window with a lightning bolt and then joke about how he's definitely fine. It's all about creative problem-solving, with each character sporting a completely unique set of skills. A necromancer medic who heals by murdering people? Sure. A storm witch who can chain-zap half the room into unconsciousness? Absolutely. A dude who literally sees the future to dodge consequences? They said it couldn't be done.

It should feel broken. It doesn't. The enemies are just as overpowered as you, and your squad members are about as durable as a wet napkin. Every level feels like walking a knife's edge, except you're also juggling and the knife is on fire. And that's what makes it brilliant. You're constantly pulling off ridiculous strategies that shouldn't work, but they do, and when they do, it's beautiful.

Solid gameplay makes it good, what really makes this game special is the tone. And that tone? It feels eerily familiar. Awfully similar to a Dungeons &

Dragons campaign where the DM has given up on keeping things balanced and is just rolling with the chaos. The world is bleak, the stakes are high, and the characters should be taking everything very seriously... but instead, they're cracking jokes, executing wildly impractical plans, and treating life-or-death situations with the same energy as someone debating whether to use their last spell slot on a fireball or a really good punchline (why not both?). It's that perfect balance of tension and levity, the exact dynamic that makes a great D&D session unforgettable. And Tactical Breach Wizards thrives on this tone.

On paper, Tactical Breach Wizards is a dark game. And I don't mean ooh, it's edgy and gritty, like a Batman reboot. No, this thing dives headfirst into a world of corrupt cops, theocratic regimes, global drug empires, and paramilitary groups that pull the strings of war and politics. The personal stakes? Also bleak. These characters have capital B Baggage. Childhood trauma, anxiety spirals, PTSD, broken loyalties, existential crises – all there, simmering beneath the surface.

And the game makes you feel it. Each character's internal struggles manifest as dreamlike combat encounters, where their fears and neuroses become mechanics you have to actually play through. These sequences are brilliant because they don't just tell you a character is struggling, they make their struggles a problem you need to solve. It's a genius way to integrate storytelling into gameplay.

So yeah, the world's a mess, the characters are broken, and yet... somehow this is one of the funniest games I've played.

The characters don't constantly engage with the horror of their world. They can't, it would lead to despair. Instead, they do what every self-respecting D&D party does in the face of overwhelming despair: they joke about it.

Before every breach (the titular primary action of the game), the team takes a second to crack wise about their increasingly absurd predicament. They snark, they tease, they make light of their own mortality. And there's an ongoing gag that no one ever actually dies. No, no, enemies are simply "stunned," "ejected from the building," or "sent to a hell dimension for an hour or two." Definitely not killed. Absolutely no moral complications here.

This dynamic is so D&D it hurts. A good campaign balances comedy and darkness exactly like this. Banter-filled moment-to-moment gameplay, interspersed with sharp dives into serious emotional depth when the time is right. A really good campaign (or in this case, game) uses that contrast to make both elements stronger. The humor makes the dark moments hit harder because they feel earned, and the dark moments give weight to the humor because we need it to get through.

Plenty of games go full grimdark, all oppressive atmosphere, no breathing room. Others go full comedy. Funny, but with no weight. This game walks the line perfectly. The world sucks, but the people in it refuse to let it break them. They cope how they can. They joke because it keeps them going. And, honestly? That feels a lot more human than either extreme.

But more than that, Tactical Breach Wizards understands something about why we play games in the first place. The best games, and the best D&D campaigns, aren't just about mechanics or plot. They're about the experience of playing. The fun of improvisation, of rolling with whatever nonsense happens, of making increasingly ridiculous plans and somehow… Somehow, pulling them off.

16

How Wildermyth Taught Me to Pretend

Most games are better when you stop playing them "correctly."

Wildermyth cracked this wide open for me. It's a game that practically begs you to lean in, let your imagination take the wheel, and start weaving little soap operas out of grid-based combat and dialogue snippets. It offers this beautifully chaotic sandbox where story just happens. Not because the game tells it, but because you, decide it matters. Let me explain.

Wildermyth sets the stage with a few clever tools. You start with three randomly generated nobodies, "farmer who once saw a squirrel carry 13 nuts at once!" type nobodies. Over the course of the campaign, you guide them through battles, choices, transformations, heartbreaks, retirements, and the occasional flaming orb grafted to their skull. It blends tactical combat with a storytelling engine that's light-touch but deceptively powerful. It throws in personality traits, relationship arcs, age progression, and a few strange, mystical modifiers, and suddenly you're watching character arcs unfold like they were pulled from a fantasy anthology.

Here's an example: in one of my runs, two women fell in love mid-campaign. Nothing explicit, no sweeping violin soundtrack, but in my mind they were definitely in love. Just some gentle scenes, a few narrative beats. Then, in middle age, one of them vanished, pursuing immortality, because of course she did. She returned decades later, unchanged and unaged, helping the team defeat a threat to the land. The romance? Long dead, 30 years can do that. But the friendship? Still kicking. Meanwhile, her ex had wandered off into the woods, befriending beasts and leant into solitude without her partner. No developer wrote that arc. No achievement unlocked. But to me? That story happened, and it was beautiful.

That's the magic of emergent storytelling. You get a pile of vague breadcrumbs, some quirks, some events, maybe a line of dialogue and your brain fills in the rest. Wildermyth is exceptional at this. It's not just emergent strategy like Civilization, where the communist George Washington Nuked the Persians to capture South East Asia. Funny, interesting but not really a character driven story. I think you can create and enhance emergent stories within any game if you use a bit of imagination, a play a tad suboptimally.

Wildermyth just makes it easy. But the same storytelling energy is buried in Civilization, XCOM, Pokemon, even Skyrim if you squint. All it takes is a little willingness to stop being a spreadsheet-loving min-max machine and start being a dumb little kid again. Take Civilisation again you can lean into the story of your undying soldier. The single warrior that barely survived a barbarian fight on turn 10, saving your worker. Then level them up throughout the entire game until they are a future infantry with 6 promotions. Throwing your whole army behind them to support and make sure they get back safe, as that forever soldier is your captain. Not strategically optimal (at all), but it makes a fun story, you just have to add your own silly goal, of keep this soldier alive.

Some people even add extra rules to games to try to force this emergent storytelling. Think of Pokemon Nuzlockes, before they became so widespread and tactical. It was all about having to nickname all your pokemon so you formed an emotional attachment, this forced more emergent stories and narratives. The Pidgey that saved the run. Or for me, the Bidoof that I thought was useless but came in clutch to beat the 3rd gym leader. Later, noblely sacrificing themselves in the 5th gym so the Luxio who had trained under them, fathered by the now evolved Bibarel could go on to sweep the gym.

To me this all just shows that you can force emergent stories into most games. It makes them more fun, compelling and exciting. It just means you have to set some hard rules for yourself, that then mean you play a tad suboptimally. It means saying "no, that wasn't just RNG" and "yes, I will avenge my fallen bearwife, hunting every goblin I hear about." It's choosing to value vibes and story over a quick win. And drama over damage output.

That's what makes Wildermyth so brilliant, it doesn't force you. It tempts you. With its little text boxes, its weird transformations, its loose threads just begging to be tied into something more. But any game can become Wildermyth if you play it that way. If you make space for your imagination to show up. If you play suboptimally, like a fool, because the fool's story is always the best one.

So next time you're gaming, try this: set your own goal. Pick a favorite unit and never let them die, no matter the cost. Invent a tragic backstory for your main character. Name your army after your childhood pets. Pretend you're back in the sandbox, inventing plots with sticks and rocks, only now there's better graphics. Turns out, pretending is still fun as hell. Especially when you're the one writing the story.

17

Demystifying the Deck: Why Card Games Are Having a Glorious Renaissance

Once upon a time, playing a card game meant dragging a folding table out of storage, arguing about house rules, and trying to ignore the suspiciously sticky spot under your uncle's chair. There was charm in it, sure. The tactile shuffle of the deck, the ritual of drawing a hand, the camaraderie (or chaos) that came with a good play. But it was a commitment. You needed the cards, the people, the time, and the patience to decode rulebooks that looked like they'd been written by a committee of particularly vengeful lawyers.

Then, card games went digital, and everything changed.

In the past few years, games like *Night of the Full Moon* and *Meteorfall* have quietly staged a revolution. They took a genre that was often dense and inaccessible, and reimagined it for the age of smartphones, headphones, and pajamas. What used to demand setup and a physical deck now lives in your pocket, ready to launch into a strategic adventure during your lunch break. And somehow, miraculously, none of the depth was lost in translation.

Night of the Full Moon is a perfect example of what this new wave of card games can do. It plays like a bedtime story narrated by someone who really,

really loves probability curves. You're weaving a dark fairy tale one card at a time. The game blends RPG elements, narrative arcs, and turn-based combat into a seamless experience that feels more like reading a choose-your-own-adventure novel than playing a card game. But underneath the fairy-tale aesthetic and slick presentation is a strategic spine made of steel. Deck-building is the core mechanic, the language through which you shape your journey.

And yet, despite all this depth, *Night of the Full Moon* is approachable. It doesn't throw you into a pit of keywords and synergies. It leads you in gently, one mechanic at a time, like a kindly forest witch offering you tea before teaching you how to hex someone. This is where the magic happens. The game keeps things intuitive enough for newcomers while offering enough variation and challenge to keep veterans intrigued. It proves that complexity doesn't have to mean confusion, and accessibility doesn't have to mean shallow.

That same philosophy pulses through *Meteorfall*, a game that looks like a Saturday morning cartoon and plays like a strategy seminar wearing a silly hat. Its entire control scheme boils down to a swipe left or right. That's it. Every choice, every action, every heroic triumph or strategic blunder happens with a simple flick of your thumb. But don't mistake that for mindless simplicity. *Meteorfall* pulls off something rare: it distills deck-building into its purest form. It trims the fat, removes the clutter, and leaves behind only the meaningful decisions. It's a game that doesn't look like it's testing you, until you realise you've been thinking three moves ahead for the last ten minutes without even noticing.

This elegant minimalism makes *Meteorfall* a near-perfect entry point for people who've never touched a deck-builder in their lives. It quietly teaches you how to think like a strategist. And then, once you're hooked, you're suddenly eyeing up more complicated games like *Slay the Spire*. But *Meteorfall* gives you the tools to survive the ascent. It's a stepping stone, a secret tutor, a friendly hand extended to newcomers saying, "Hey. You can do this."

What ties *Night of the Full Moon* and *Meteorfall* together isn't just that they're great games (though they are), but that they understand what makes deck-building magical in the first place. It's not about rare cards or fancy combos or understanding twelve types of damage mitigation. It's about choice. It's about being handed a random set of tools and figuring out, on the fly, how to turn them into something powerful. That core experience: improvising, adapting, learning from failure, and finally pulling off a perfect win is what makes card games so enduring.

By translating that into digital form, these games have done more than just modernise an old genre. They've democratised it. You no longer need a friend group fluent in game mechanics or a shelf full of expansions to enjoy a great card game. You just need a phone and a willingness to think. And the best part? These games haven't sacrificed their complexity to do it. They've simply hidden it behind smoother interfaces, better pacing, and a little bit of style.

This shift is a statement. It says that strategy can be sleek. That depth doesn't have to be buried under jargon. That you can make hard decisions with a smile on your face, and that maybe, just maybe, a deck-building game can feel more like a storybook than a spreadsheet.

So here's to the new age of digital card games. To swiping instead of shuffling. To complex systems disguised as casual fun. To the kind of games that sneak up on you, teach you to think differently, and then have the audacity to be beautiful. Whether you're building decks in the haunted woods of *Night of the Full Moon* or swiping your way through *Meteorfall*'s absurd dungeon crawl, you're part of a genre that's evolving. Not by locking new players out, but by inviting them in.

18

Monster Train and Matrix Design

Some games feel like they were designed by mad scientists trying to cram in as many mechanics as possible. Others strip things down to their bare bones, hoping that minimalism alone can carry the experience. Monster Train does something different. It builds a deep, strategic experience not by adding complexity, but by layering simple mechanics into a vast web of possibilities. I call this matrix design, and it's the reason Monster Train is one of the most repayable and engaging deck-builders out there.

At its core, Monster Train is a roguelike deck-builder. You play cards to summon units, cast spells, and defend your pyre as waves of enemies ascend through the floors of your train. The core gameplay loop is simple and easy to grasp. But here's where it gets interesting: Monster Train doesn't rely on sheer randomness or vast card pools to create variety. Instead, it builds depth through structured choices that interact in ways that are both predictable and surprising. The magic of this design comes from its dual-class system. Unlike Slay the Spire, the icon and gold standard for the genre, where each run starts with one of four characters. Monster Train lets you pick a primary and a secondary clan. With five clans total, that's ten possible starting class combinations right off the bat. But it doesn't stop there.

Each clan has two different champions, and you can only use a champion from your primary class. That means that for every class combination, there are two different champion builds available, resulting in 40 different champion-secondary class combinations. And if that wasn't enough, each secondary class also comes with two possible starter card sets, effectively doubling the variations to 80 different configurations. All that variety is before any randomness even kicks in.

Now compare that to Slay the Spire. You get four characters. That's it. Once you pick a character, randomness decides the rest. In Monster Train, you sculpt your run from the start with meaningful choices that shape how you play. The moment-to-moment action might feel more consistent, but the sheer breadth of starting scenarios makes every run feel fresh.

This is where Monster Train and Slay the Spire diverge the most. In Slay the Spire, runs often feel like an exercise in executing a build you already know, especially on higher difficulty. There's skill in navigating the chaos, you're playing the odds, steering the ship and hoping the wind is in your favor.

Monster Train, on the other hand, embraces consistency. You always start with a champion who is guaranteed to be in your hand. You always have relatively consistent and regular upgrade options for your units and spells. Every run gives you a sense of control that Slay the Spire lacks. The balance here is delicate: the game is structured enough to avoid frustration, but flexible enough to keep things interesting.

The real genius of Monster Train is how it achieves this depth without making the game overwhelming. Every run starts with a limited set of choices. Two to be exact, your champion and your secondary clan, but these choices multiply exponentially because every element works together. This is what I mean by matrix design, instead of just stacking more and more mechanics on top of each other, Monster Train takes a handful of core mechanics and lets them interact in every possible way. I mean every possible way. Every combination of champion and secondary is functional and feels unique. You can visualise it all in a huge matrix table of champion-clan combinations (hence the name). The result is a game that is both approachable and endlessly replayable.

This approach keeps the gameplay simple while maximising variety. Each class, champion, and upgrade works within the same framework, ensuring that everything feels cohesive.

Another thing Monster Train does exceptionally well is making every run feel worthwhile. In Slay the Spire, failing a run can feel like you just got unlucky. Maybe the right relic never showed up, or maybe you never found the right synergy. The game's depth comes from its massive deck and relic variety, but that also means a lot of your success is out of your hands.

In Monster Train, failure usually feels like it was your fault. Because of the matrix design, you always have a clear idea of what your deck could do. You can predict the power curve of your units. You can plan around your champion's abilities. You can decide whether you want to lean into spells, units, or a balanced strategy. Every decision has weight, and that makes failure feel like a learning experience rather than just bad luck.

What makes Monster Train a masterpiece isn't its complexity, it's the way it extracts maximum depth from a simple framework. You don't need thousands of cards, dozens of relics, or an encyclopedic knowledge of synergies. Instead, the game presents a structured sandbox where a small set of variables combine in fascinating ways.

Every run is different, not because of blind luck, but because you chose for it to be different. Until you start replaying class combinations, every single run is a new puzzle. And even then, because of the flexible upgrade system, the same class combination can play wildly differently depending on what you prioritise.

This is why Monster Train never feels stale. It doesn't bombard you with complexity, it invites you to explore a beautifully interconnected system where every decision matters.

19

Peglin's Role in the Evolution of Hybrid Games

In the vast, mystical forest of video games, where paths cross and genres intertwine like ancient roots, a curious creature named Peglin has emerged. Peglin, with its unique combination of pinball mechanics, RPG elements, and rogue-like progression, stands at the forefront of a shift to hybrid games, illustrating the potential for genre fusion to create novel gaming experiences. Peglin's gameplay mechanics and genre-blending approach contribute to its role as a pioneer in the hybrid game movement, appealing to a diverse audience and influencing the broader gaming landscape.

Peglin demonstrates how integrating the simple, skill-based gameplay of pinball with the strategic depth of role-playing games can result in a compelling game experience. The pinball mechanics offer an accessible entry point for casual gamers, reminiscent of arcade classics, yet the addition of RPG elements like upgrades, abilities, and a varied arsenal of orbs introduces a layer of strategy typically reserved for more hardcore gaming experiences.

The strategic depth in Peglin arises from the player's need to choose the right orbs (each with unique abilities) for their playthrough, plan their shots to maximise damage, and adapt their strategy based on the randomly generated encounter pathways. This blend of strategy and skill appeals to a wide range of players, from those who enjoy the tactile satisfaction of pinball to those who prefer the thoughtful planning of RPGs.

Peglin's incorporation of rogue-like elements further enriches its gameplay, adding a layer of unpredictability and replayability that is a hallmark to the genre. The game's semi-random ordering of levels and encounters ensures that no two playthroughs are the same, challenging players to adapt their strategies in real-time and learn from each attempt. This unpredictability not only extends the game's longevity but also taps into the human desire for challenge and mastery, appealing to gamers who thrive on overcoming difficult and ever-changing obstacles. Moreover, the rogue-like progression system, where players gradually unlock new orbs and abilities that can appear in subsequent runs, encourages experimentation and discovery. This system rewards persistence and learning, core aspects of rogue-like games, and introduces a sense of progression and growth that keeps players engaged.

Peglin's success in blending genres signals a broader trend towards hybridisation in game design, challenging traditional genre boundaries and encouraging innovation. By successfully merging elements from distinct genres, Peglin demonstrates the potential for hybrid games to offer rich, multifaceted experiences that cater to diverse player preferences and interests.

This genre blending also suggests a shift in how developers and players perceive games, moving away from rigid categorisations towards a more fluid understanding of game mechanics and experiences. It highlights the potential for creative freedom in game design, where developers can draw from a broad palette of mechanics and themes to craft unique experiences.

Peglin's role in the rise of hybrid games is emblematic of a larger movement in the gaming industry towards innovation, diversity, and the breaking down of traditional genre barriers. Its unique combination of pinball, RPG, and rogue-like elements not only offers a fresh and engaging player experience but also serves as a case study in how blending genres can appeal to a wide audience and enrich the gaming landscape. As the gaming industry continues to evolve, Peglin's contribution to the hybrid game genre will likely be seen as a pivotal moment in encouraging developers to explore new combinations of gameplay mechanics, themes, and experiences.

20

Rolling the Dice: The Tension and Transparency of Randomness in 'Slice and Dice'

In the gaming world, the charm of roguelikes and the unpredictable nature of a simple six-sided dice share a common thread: the thrilling unpredictability they bring. This essay explores how the transparent randomness of a six-sided dice, a concept familiar even to those with the most rudimentary understanding of games, magnifies the inherent randomness of roguelikes, making their complexity more accessible and, ultimately, enhancing the gaming experience.

Roguelikes, characterised by their procedural generation and permadeath, are a genre that thrives on unpredictability. Every playthrough offers a new maze of dungeons, assortments of loot, and encounters with foes, ensuring that no two games are ever the same. This level of variability can be daunting, as players must continuously adapt their strategies without any guarantee of what lies ahead. Herein lies the genius of integrating the straightforward randomness of a six-sided dice into the fabric of roguelike games, including "Slice and Dice."

A six-sided dice is, perhaps, the epitome of randomness encapsulated in a tangible form. Each roll is a straightforward gamble, with outcomes ranging from one to six, each with an equal chance of occurrence. This simplicity makes the concept of randomness easily graspable, players understand that their fate is at the mercy of chance with every roll. When this type of randomness is woven into the mechanics of a roguelike game, it serves as an anchor to the more complex layers of randomness that define the genre.

By incorporating dice-based randomness, roguelikes like "Slice and Dice" manage to make the unpredictability of their worlds more approachable. Players may not always grasp the intricate algorithms that dictate the procedural generation of levels or item spawns, but they can understand the immediate, visible randomness of a dice roll. This comprehension bridges the gap between the player and the game's deeper complexities, making the experience more engaging. The dice become a metaphor for the game's randomness, providing a clear, comprehensible example of how chance impacts gameplay.

The act of rolling a dice introduces a tactile sense of anticipation and excitement, a brief moment where outcomes are suspended in the air, much like the uncertain prospects in a roguelike dungeon. This enhances player engagement and investment in each decision and its consequences. The clear and present randomness of the dice roll adds a layer of strategy and risk assessment, as players must weigh their actions against the potential outcomes dictated by chance. The dice roll serves as a constant reminder of the stakes. In a genre where every choice can lead to glory or doom, the tangible randomness of the dice underscores the precariousness of the player's journey. This not only amplifies the tension and excitement but also deepens the player's connection to the game, as they navigate through a world where fortune and fate are inextricably linked.

Incorporating the randomness of six-sided dice into the mechanics of roguelike games like "Slice and Dice" achieves more than just an additional layer of chance. It makes the inherent unpredictability of the genre more accessible and comprehensible to players, thereby enhancing their engagement and enjoyment. Through the simple roll of a dice, the complex and often opaque randomness of roguelikes is distilled into a form that players can easily understand and appreciate, transforming the gaming experience into one that is as exhilarating as it is unpredictable.

21

The Joy of "Working" in Satisfactory

At first glance, Satisfactory might look like a productivity simulator posing as a game. It's all about efficiency, logistics, and managing resources. Tasks that, in the real world, sound suspiciously like, well, work. Yet players (like me) keep coming back. Spending hours refining layouts, optimising production lines, and expanding their factory empires across alien landscapes. So why does this virtual work feel so much more fulfilling and enjoyable than the many tasks of everyday life?

The answer lies in how Satisfactory takes the concept of "work" and reframes it to tap into deep psychological rewards. While real-life work is often fraught with stress, delays, and unpredictability, Satisfactory presents a vision of work that is predictable, rewarding, and thoroughly satisfying (haha, get it).

One of the most compelling aspects of Satisfactory is how it transforms progress into something that is not just achievable but inevitable. In real life, every project comes with its own share of obstacles: random meetings, delays, unexpected mistakes, and just plain human error. The process is rarely smooth, and there's often no clear end in sight. In Satisfactory, however, every resource you need is there for the taking, and every task directly contributes to your larger goal. You mine ore, produce parts, and build machines that work exactly as expected, every time. There's no chance that your iron smelter will suddenly break down, no threat of a logistics failure, and no unexpected setbacks to derail your work. If any of these things do happen, it's because of your factory design and the cause is transparent. Oh, the power shut down. Oh the machine says it's only running at 50% because it lacks iron rods. This sense of clear, reliable progress is incredibly satisfying because it strips away the uncertainty that so often saps motivation in the real world.

In Satisfactory, work becomes a straightforward path to achievement. Every new production tier, completed project, and optimised conveyor belt brings a tangible sense of advancement that feels like a job well done. You're building something that grows bigger and better with every effort you put into it. And unlike the unpredictability of real-life work, where a project can suddenly veer off in a different direction, Satisfactory offers stability. You get to see your plans come to fruition without interference, making every completed task feel like a genuine accomplishment.

Work rarely lets us control every detail in this way. We might have to answer to a boss, collaborate with a team, or adjust our efforts based on shifting priorities. Satisfactory removes all these variables, placing you in charge of every choice, every design, and every task. The freedom to control your factory layout, production lines, resource allocation. Hell, even if you just want to explore for a few hours. This gives players a rare sense of complete autonomy.

You create the workspace itself. Every conveyor belt, every smelter, and every production line is entirely up to you. This level of agency transforms the experience from task fulfilment to something much closer to personal expression. Are you a ball of chaotic mess (like myself) and have conveyors doubling back in every direction, a strict one production line policy, or something else that suits you. You're not just following orders or adapting to someone else's design; you're building your ideal system, one that matches your vision of how everything should flow and function. This power over every detail gives players a unique sense of ownership, as if they're crafting the perfect work environment that's always within their control.

Efficiency is often the name of the game in real-world work, but it's usually accompanied by high stakes and tight deadlines. The pressure to optimise or "do more with less" can create stress rather than satisfaction, especially when failure has real consequences. In Satisfactory, however, efficiency is a personal goal rather than a demand. There's no looming boss, no deadline, and no risk of reprimand if your layout isn't perfect. You can spend hours refining a production line just for the sake of seeing it run smoothly, without any external pressure pushing you to get it done faster.

This freedom to pursue efficiency at your own pace allows players to experience the joys of optimisation without the stress. You're not optimising to please anyone else, you're doing it purely for the pleasure of seeing everything work seamlessly. Each time you adjust a conveyor belt, reposition a machine, or refine a layout, you're rewarded with the visual and operational payoff of a smoother, faster system. It's as if the game takes the best part of efficiency, the satisfaction of improvement, without any of the associated stress. There's a deep contentment I feel watching a factory reach peak efficiency, and that's magnified by the fact that I can take as much or as little time as I like to achieve it.

As you progress in Satisfactory, the complexity of your production lines grows exponentially. Where you once managed a simple iron ore line, you now juggle multiple resources, complex recipes, and power grids that span vast areas. This complexity brings the joy of problem-solving, with every new production level presenting fresh challenges to tackle. Yet unlike real life, where complexity often leads to frustration, Satisfactory keeps its challenges manageable, and failure is never catastrophic.

There's no penalty for failure, which makes experimentation feel safe and even encouraged. Everything in Satisfactory can be demolished and give you 100% of the resources back. You're free to try a wild new layout, reroute your power grid, or redesign your entire factory without fearing negative consequences. A factory running at 10% is still producing things that will help you, this makes everything progress even when it doesn't work. The stakes are low, and this freedom to fail lets you embrace the complexity as a fun puzzle rather than an anxiety-inducing risk. You get to grapple with each challenge as it comes, knowing that you can always tweak, adjust, or even start over if something doesn't work as expected.

This setup is incredibly freeing. It allows players to explore complex systems and test their problem-solving skills without any of the usual anxieties that real-life projects can bring. The result is a form of "work" that feels challenging but not overwhelming. A kind of mental playground where you can test ideas, improve upon them, and create solutions that feel like pure accomplishments.

There's a unique kind of joy in seeing everything come together. When your factory is humming along, with every machine running at peak efficiency, every resource feeding smoothly into production, and every power line perfectly connected, or if you are me, none of the above (but I still get the job done). Regardless, it creates a feeling of accomplishment that's difficult to replicate. You've managed to create order from chaos, designing a system that's both functional and (sometimes) elegant.

This satisfaction is rooted in the idea that you've taken raw resources, complex recipes, and your own ingenuity, and created something that runs like a well-oiled machine. In real life, creating such harmony often requires overcoming endless obstacles: budget cuts, deadlines, competing priorities, and random mishaps. In Satisfactory, however, you can achieve this harmony on your own terms, and the result is a pure, distilled sense of achievement that comes from seeing your system working just as you intended.

In essence, Satisfactory takes the concept of "work" and transforms it into something deeply enjoyable by stripping away the frustrations, unpredictability, and consequences that often make real-life work feel draining. In this world, work becomes a creative, rewarding, and endlessly engaging activity.

The game allows you to experience the joy of progress, the thrill of efficiency, and the satisfaction of problem-solving, all without the usual burdens of stress, time constraints, or the need to meet someone else's expectations. In doing so, it manages to turn "work" into something that players not only enjoy but seek out, proving that when work is stripped down to its most engaging elements, it can become a source of pure, unadulterated satisfaction.

22

Redline: Burn Everything

If you haven't seen *Redline*, stop reading. Go watch it. Right now. Don't ask what it's about, because explaining it is like trying to describe the taste of adrenaline. This movie is a shot of pure, uncut madness. Cars that scream past at Mach Jesus, explosions every 15 seconds, and a plot that exists solely to string together scenes of characters who look like they've been pulled from a fever dream of *Mad Max* and *JoJo's Bizarre Adventure*. It's not a movie you watch; it's a movie you survive. And holy shit, it's worth it.

But here's the kicker: *Redline* wasn't just a movie. It was a declaration. A dare. A kamikaze dive of creativity that came at an absurd cost – financially, physically, and emotionally – to everyone involved. This masterpiece of chaos was brought to life by Madhouse, a studio with a track record of animating some of the wildest and most stylish shows of all time. We're talking *Trigun*, *Ninja Scroll*, and *Perfect Blue*. But *Redline*? It wasn't just a project. It was their magnum opus, their love letter to animation, and their financial death knell.

Redline took seven years to make. Seven. Years. Do you know what was happening seven years before *Redline* premiered in 2011? George W. Bush was still president, the iPhone didn't exist, and *Shrek* 2 was considered peak cinema. Madhouse spent the better part of a decade hand-drawing every single frame of this beast, committing to the kind of detailed, balls-to-the-wall animation that other studios abandoned when they realised CGI was cheaper and faster. But Madhouse didn't give a shit about cheap or fast. They wanted capital A Art. They wanted *Redline*.

The director, Takeshi Koike, helmed this passion project with the determination of a man who eats crayons for breakfast and calls it a balanced diet. Koike's vision was simple: create the coolest, most intense, most visually stunning animated movie ever. Subtlety? Fuck subtlety. Plot coherence? Who needs it? This wasn't about telling a story; it was about turning the medium of animation into a flamethrower aimed directly at your brain.

And damn, did they deliver. The result is a movie that looks like a comic book decided to take steroids, got addicted, and started hanging out with the Fast & Furious crew. Thick, bold black lines outline every character and vehicle, giving the animation a raw, almost aggressive energy. The colors are neon fever dreams, the camera angles are borderline absurd, and the sound design? It's like a rock concert, an engine roar, and a screaming crowd had a love child and then cranked the volume to 11.

The plot of *Redline* is laughably simple: a death race on a planet full of aliens, corrupt politicians, and a sentient bioweapon or two. But it doesn't matter. The movie isn't about the why; it's about the how. Every second is engineered to make you feel like you've been shot out of a cannon. The races don't just look fast; they feel fast. The screen shakes, the engines roar, and the camera practically breaks its neck trying to keep up with the action. You don't care if the physics make sense, because you're too busy screaming at the sheer audacity of what's happening.

Redline is pure, unfiltered style. It doesn't care about realism or logic or whether your eardrums survive the experience. It cares about being cool. And that's what makes it so goddamn brilliant. It's a movie that understands the value of spectacle. Every frame, every sound, every insane twist is designed to make your jaw hit the floor. Watching *Redline* is like riding shotgun with a driver who has zero regard for the brakes. It's reckless, and it's glorious.

But perfection has a price, and *Redline* paid it in full. Madhouse poured everything into this movie: money, time, and the sanity of its animators. By the time it finally premiered, it was clear that the studio had overextended itself. *Redline* bombed at the box office, earning just a fraction of what it cost to make. Critics loved it, fans adored it, but the general public didn't show up. It's a tragic irony. The movie that's all about going all-in ended up bankrupting the very studio that made it.

But maybe that's fitting. *Redline* isn't the kind of movie that could have been made by playing it safe. It's a passion project in the truest sense, a movie that exists because a team of insane geniuses decided to ignore the rules and go for broke. And in doing so, they created something timeless. Something unforgettable.

At its core, *Redline* is about the pursuit of style. It's about going fast, looking cool, and giving zero fucks about anything else. The movie itself mirrors the ethos of its protagonist, JP, a racer who risks everything to win. Not because he has to, but because he loves it. That's what *Redline* is. It's not trying to teach you a lesson or make you think. It's here to blow your mind, melt your face, and remind you that sometimes, the only thing that matters is how cool something looks and feels.

So yeah, *Redline* killed Madhouse's wallet. But it also gave us one of the most insane, jaw-dropping, and stylish pieces of animation ever created. It's a testament to what can happen when you throw caution to the wind and let pure creativity take the wheel.

And damn it, that's worth every penny.

23

This Is Not a Bar (But It Fucking Is): Surrealism Meets Sincerity With Nathan Fielder

Nathan Fielder is either the most emotionally intelligent weirdo on TV, or the most socially oblivious genius to ever walk into a room backwards while narrating his own internal monologue. The Rehearsal, his HBO acid trip disguised as a docu-reality series, is what happens when a man is given unlimited resources, a blank check from a prestige network, and absolutely no adult supervision. It's both art and prank, therapy and punishment. It's like watching someone try to clone human empathy in a Petri dish.

And it's fucking surreal.

From the jump, Nathan's premise is already batshit: help people prepare for major life events by recreating them in absurdly accurate simulations. Not just like "let's roleplay" accurate. No, no, no, we're talking carbon copy sets, background actors trained for weeks, flow charts of possible conversation branches.

But then things spiral (of course they do).

At the heart of The Rehearsal is this rabbit hole of identity that Nathan keeps falling down, hitting every metal pipe of emotional repression on the way. Is TV Nathan just a bit? A persona? A cracked mirror of the real guy? There are moments, like when a child actor (one of many rotating child actors, because of labor laws, of course) starts to actually see Nathan as his father, and the mask starts slipping. Or maybe it doesn't. Maybe that's just another layer. Maybe the vulnerability is the bit. Maybe nothing is real and we're all just cardboard cutouts drinking in the fake bar with the 80-foot hallway entrance. Which again, functions as a bar, has regulars, and a liquor license, but also... is not real. It's a fake bar... That's real. What the fuck?

It's the Magritte pipe but with beer and LED lighting. This is not a bar. But it IS a bar. It's like Nathan stared at the absurdity of modern life and decided the best way to fight it was to build a diorama of it using tweezers and madness.

And then there's The Fielder Method episode, which is where he teaches actors how to "be" the real people they're pretending to be in these simulations. So now we have actors rehearsing being people who are rehearsing being themselves. Then Nathan decides he needs to better understand the father-son relationship he's simulating, so he rehearses being himself by hiring an actor to play the version of himself that other people see. There are more Nathans on screen than there are answers, and somehow each one is more emotionally constipated than the last.

And that's kind of the beauty of the whole thing: it's a comedy show that actively resists being laughed at. It's funny, sure; but, the kind of funny that makes you feel complicit and deeply worried. Like you're watching something sacred and profane at the same time. It's a magic trick that slowly turns into a therapy session, and then suddenly, it's a hostage situation where you're the one tied up by your own thoughts.

I don't even know how to feel about this show. It's art, but it's also an anxiety attack wrapped in high production values. It's for people who like their entertainment with a side of philosophical dread. Or a surreal trainwreck of someone quietly unraveling over six episodes while trying to simulate perfect parenting with a six-year-old and then a grown man pretending to be a six-year-old... If that excites you, yeah, this one's for you.

So would I recommend The Rehearsal? Yes. But only if you're ready to have your brain cracked open like a fortune cookie written by Kafka. Bring snacks. Bring a therapist. And maybe rehearse watching it a few times before you actually press play.

24

Life's a Joke, and Then You Cry: The Tragicomedy of Diary of an Uber Driver

There's a specific kind of comedy that Diary of an Uber Driver nails. Dry, deadpan, slightly bleak but deeply human storytelling that captures the weirdness of life without making a big deal about it. It's not some grand reinvention of the genre, but it is good. Good in the way a quiet moment with a stranger can be unexpectedly meaningful. Good in the way a passing comment can stick with you for years. Good in the way life is sometimes just stupid and awkward and funny and sad all at once. I love this kind of storytelling.

British and Australian comedy seems to have a particular knack for it. Shows like After Life, Please Like Me, Fleabag, and Diary of an Uber Driver all operate in this space between tragedy and humor, between the profound and the ridiculous. They don't force a laugh every thirty seconds, and they don't pander to an audience desperate for a neat emotional resolution. They just observe life, in all its weird, lonely, absurd beauty, and let us sit with it.

These shows thrive on contrast. One minute, they'll have you deeply invested in a character's personal struggle, and the next, they'll completely undercut it with a throwaway comment that punctures the drama. Not in a way that makes the emotional moment feel cheap, but in a way that highlights how life rarely plays out like a well-structured movie.

Take the B plot of an uber passenger who is an architect in Diary of an Uber Driver. He doesn't want to talk in the car. He's just another closed-off, emotionally unavailable passenger. Then we see him later, staring out his opulently minimalist apartment window, seeing an old man collapsed in a chair, maybe he's dead? The scene builds up all the weight of a moral dilemma: should he intervene? Should he care? When he finally takes action, it's this huge, cathartic moment of human connection. And then after hours of trying to get to this man, in tears at his door… the old man miraculously opens it, "fuck off you poof… SLAM!"

That moment? That's life. We reach out. We make an effort. We put ourselves out there. And sometimes, we just get metaphorically smacked in the face for it. But instead of turning that into a moment of despair, the show makes it funny. Because what else can you do?

This is why these shows work so well for me—they don't just point out the absurdity of life; they highlight the way that absurdity is what makes life interesting. They're not about huge, world-changing events. They're about people existing in the quiet spaces in between. A young man navigating the awkward mess of adulthood while dealing with mental health, heartbreak, and the general chaos of human relationships (Please Like Me). A sharp, self-destructive woman deflecting her grief and guilt with wit and bad decisions while trying (and failing) to be better (Fleabag). A grieving man just trying to get through the day (After Life). And, of course, an Uber driver, cycling through endless fleeting connections, trying to make sense of his own life in the process.

These shows don't treat their characters like heroes. They're just people. Flawed, messy, sometimes terrible, sometimes wonderful people. And that's why they feel so real. They show us how lonely people can be, even when they're surrounded by others. How much we all crave connection, even when we pretend we don't. How ridiculous it is to try to find meaning in a world that doesn't really owe us one.

A lot of people talk about dark comedy like it's just a way to push boundaries, but that's not really what draws me to it. What I love is the way it acknowledges that life is dark sometimes. That we all go through things that are unfair and painful and impossible to make sense of. But instead of treating that as something to mourn, these shows remind us that sometimes, the best thing we can do is laugh at it.

Not in a dismissive way. Not in a way that minimises the pain. But in a way that recognises the humor in how ridiculous it all is. The way desperation makes people contradict themselves. The way self-awareness doesn't always translate into self-control. The way failure is sometimes the most relatable thing in the world.

There's a moment in Diary of an Uber Driver where Ben, after spending weeks bugging his ex about their unborn child, finally tells her he's backing off. He won't pressure her anymore. Won't insert himself into her life. He makes it sound like a revelation, like he's grown. And then, of course, that same night, he's back at her doorstep. It's a perfect moment of human contradiction—earnest in intention, doomed in execution.

But the show doesn't pause for some big emotional reckoning. There's no breakthrough, no dramatic shift in their dynamic. It just... moves on. Because that's what people do. They make promises they can't keep, they try to be better and fail immediately, they say one thing and do another. And it's frustrating, but also hilarious.

This kind of humor works for me because it's honest. It doesn't pretend that everything makes sense or that there's always a lesson to be learned. It doesn't shy away from sadness or awkwardness or failure. But it also doesn't wallow in them. It just lets them exist, side by side with laughter.

That's why I love Diary of an Uber Driver and shows like it. Not because they're revolutionary, but because they're real. Because they find meaning in the smallest, dumbest, most human moments. Because they remind us that no matter how messy life gets, there's always something to laugh about. Even if, sometimes, that something is just an old man slamming the door in your face.

25

Aussie Humor Through Fisk: The the Inner-City Comedians' Comedy

Australia has a knack for crafting comedies that feel hyper-local yet universally hilarious, blending self-deprecation, dry wit, and a fondness for absurdity with the kind of authenticity that feels like catching up with old friends. Fisk, a standout in this uniquely Aussie genre, is a sharp example of this comedic tradition, a show where every scene is steeped in the hilariously bleak charm of suburban office life. The brilliance of Fisk doesn't exist in isolation. It's part of a broader tradition of what I'm calling the "Inner-City Comedians' Comedy," a loose genre of Australian TV that features ensembles of iconic local comedians and leans into a distinctly Aussie brand of humor. Shows like Please Like Me and Rosehaven are siblings in this quirky, sardonic comedy family.

Australian humor thrives on three pillars: self-deprecation, dry wit, and the absurd. Fisk captures these pillars perfectly:

Self-deprecation as a national sport
   Australians love to take the mickey out of themselves, and Fisk leans hard into this. Helen Tudor-Fisk, played by Kitty Flanagan, is the quintessential self-deprecating Aussie: blunt, socially awkward, and perpetually under-

dressed. She's not an underdog hero fighting against injustice, she's just trying to survive the indignities of life in a job she doesn't particularly want. Her failures are hilarious because they feel painfully familiar, whether it's navigating awkward small talk or dealing with passive-aggressive coworkers.

Wit as dry as the desert

If British humor is a drizzle of sarcasm, Australian humor is a blazing sun of understatement. Fisk is filled with moments where the humor comes from what isn't said: awkward silences, sidelong glances, and the resigned tone of someone explaining yet another bureaucratic absurdity. Fisk's deadpan reactions to her colleagues and clients perfectly capture this dry, no-frills comedic style.

An affinity for the absurd

The world of probate law might not sound like fertile ground for comedy, but Fisk finds gold in its inherent weirdness. From bizarre wills to eccentric clients, the show highlights the strange rituals and small-town oddities of life that Australians love to lampoon. This isn't Veep-style political satire or the glossy hijinks of an American sitcom; it's about the absurdity of normal people being, well, people.

Fisk is the latest addition to a lineage of Australian shows that showcase ensembles of iconic comedians playing quirky characters in hyper-specific settings. This "Inner-City Comedians' Comedy" is marked by its emphasis on authenticity, small-scale storytelling, and a rotating cast of recognisable comic talent. Shows like Please Like Me (created by and starring Josh Thomas) and Rosehaven (co-created by Luke McGregor and Celia Pacquola) are prime examples of this genre. Here's what ties these shows together:

In Fisk, Kitty Flanagan is joined by a cast of comedic heavyweights like Julia Zemiro and Marty Sheargold. Similarly, Rosehaven thrives on the chemistry between Celia Pacquola and Luke McGregor, while Please Like Me combines Josh Thomas's offbeat humor with performances from veteran actors and up-and-coming comedians. These shows feel like the comedy world's version of a jam session, where each performer's unique style adds to the mix.

While Fisk is set in suburban Melbourne, Rosehaven brings the charm of rural Tasmania to life, and Please Like Me focuses on the inner-city cafes and sharehouses of Melbourne. These shows are deeply rooted in their settings, but their humor translates because they capture universally relatable experiences, awkward family dinners, the frustration of dealing with bureaucracy, and the comforting absurdity of small-town life.

There's a DIY charm to these shows, with their modest budgets and unpretentious storytelling. Fisk looks like an actual law office, not a designer's idea of one. This grounded aesthetic gives the humor room to breathe, making every awkward interaction and deadpan line feel more authentic.

The humor in Fisk and its genre cousins feels closer to British comedy than to the slick, punchline-driven style of American sitcoms. Like The Office (UK), these Australian shows find humor in awkwardness and the mundanity of daily life. But where British humor often leans into cynicism, Australian humor balances the dryness with a sense of warmth and camaraderie. It's not about mean-spirited takedowns; it's about laughing with, not at, the characters.

Compared to American comedies like Parks and Recreation, which thrive on fast-paced dialogue and larger-than-life characters, Fisk feels quieter and more introspective. The humor isn't in grand gestures or zippy one-liners; it's in the small, specific moments - like an awful $1 corner shop coffee being the most consistent caffeine Fisk can get her hands on.

The "Inner-City Comedians' Comedy" celebrates the imperfections of life in a way that feels uniquely Australian. These shows don't glamorise their settings or characters; they revel in awkwardness, find humor in failure, and honor the small victories that make life bearable. They make you laugh because you recognise yourself in the characters' struggles. In that laughter, they remind us that no matter how messy or absurd life gets, it's those imperfect moments that make it worth watching, and worth living.

26

The Grey of Apple Cider Vinegar

Most stories demand clarity. They tell us who to root for, who to hate, and who will ultimately redeem themselves. Apple Cider Vinegar denies us that comfort. Instead, it drags us into the mess, the tangled space where people don't just make bad decisions: they make understandable ones that are also terrible. They love deeply and hurt deeply. They convince themselves they're doing the right thing while causing irreversible damage. It's a portrait of flawed people, desperately trying to control their lives, even as they destroy them.

At the core of this web is Belle Gibson, the woman whose fraudulence drives the narrative. She builds a brand on deception, claiming to have cured her cancer with alternative medicine. It's easy to despise her: she manipulates, she profits off suffering, she lies. But the show doesn't let us settle into that disgust so easily. Belle doesn't cackle in the shadows, she believes in her own story. She loves her son. She clings to the version of herself that has power and meaning. The same fantasy she sells to others is one she needs for herself. She is a master manipulator, but also a person drowning in her own illusions. Her tragedy is that she's both a predator and a victim of her own making.

Then there's Milla, a real cancer patient who desperately searches for hope in places where it doesn't exist. She doesn't fake her illness: she lives it, breathes it, fights against it. But in her desperation for control, she chooses a different kind of lie. The comforting kind. She turns away from traditional medicine and embraces alternative treatments, clinging to the idea that belief alone can save her. She isn't malicious. She's not trying to con anyone. But she spreads a dangerous message. She's both a cautionary tale and a heartbreakingly human one. We want to protect her, but we also know she won't let us.

Belle's husband, Clive, exists in a state of quiet torment. He isn't oblivious to Belle's lies. He sees the inconsistencies. He must know, deep down, that none of this is real. And yet, he stays. Why? Because in this mess of deception, there's one undeniable truth. He loves Belle's child, a child that isn't his. He's not a villain, but he's not blameless either. He benefits from the fraud, even as it eats away at him. He enables Belle's lies, even as he suffers under them. His existence in the grey is particularly agonising because his love is real, even when everything else is false.

Chanelle, Belle's friend-turned-assistant, embodies a slow kind of moral decay. She doesn't start as a liar. She doesn't start as a manipulator. She's drawn into Belle's orbit because she believes in the message, in the hope it offers. But over time, the cracks become unavoidable. She sees the inconsistencies, the impossibilities. She stays anyway. Not because she wants to hurt anyone, but because admitting the truth would mean admitting she was complicit. When she finally pulls away, it's not a clean break. She isn't a hero. She's just another person who got in too deep.

And then there's Tamara, Milla's mother. She knows, on some level, that her daughter's choices are flawed. She knows these alternative treatments won't work. But she stands by her anyway. Not because she believes, but because she refuses to let Milla walk that path alone. When it is her turn to face illness, she makes the same choices. Not because she thinks they'll save her, but because that is what love means to her: standing by, even when it's wrong. It's painful, it's misguided, and it's utterly, devastatingly human.

Even the journalist investigating Belle's fraud can't escape the moral wreckage. He wants the truth. He believes in exposing deception. But his wife, like Milla, has put her faith in alternative medicine. His fight for truth isn't just professional, it's personal, a battle between principle and love. When he pulls at the threads of Belle's story, he unravels his own marriage. Is he doing the right thing? Yes. Is it destroying something he cares about? Also yes. There is no victory here, just the relentless tension of choosing between what is right and what keeps you whole.

Apple Cider Vinegar refuses to give us the satisfaction of clear resolutions. There are no triumphant moments where characters realise the error of their ways and make perfect choices. There are no true heroes, just people doing the best they can with the broken tools they have. And in that way, it is one of the most honest pieces of storytelling. It forces us to confront the truth that we all exist in some version of this grey space. That we all justify our mistakes, that we all carry contradictions. That love, belief, and desperation can lead us to do both terrible and beautiful things. And that, sometimes, there is no fixing it. Only living in it.

27

The Power of Distraction: How "Everything is Perfect" Keeps Readers Blind to Inner Turmoil

Maxine Fawcett's novel *Everything is Perfect* is a masterclass in narrative misdirection. On the surface, it's a rollicking romp of cringe-worthy escapades and steamy encounters. But lurking beneath this frothy exterior is a dark current of emotional turmoil and manic behaviour. Fawcett deftly uses the power of distraction to keep readers entertained and slightly off-balance, so when the protagonist's inner struggles are finally revealed, it hits like a fridge thrown off the empire state building.

The protagonist, Cassie, seems to lead a life filled with awkward situations and eyebrow-raising romantic escapades. One memorable scene has her attending a school function where she gets increasingly drunk and injures her children's principal. The reader can't help but laugh and cringe in equal measure. These moments are meticulously crafted to be both entertaining and distracting. You find yourself so wrapped up in Cassie's immediate predicament that you don't stop to think about why she keeps finding herself in these situations.

The novel doesn't shy away from steamy scenes either. Cassie's romantic escapades are equal parts passionate and cringeworthy disastrous. These moments are charged with enough sexual tension to keep readers hooked, but they also serve a deeper purpose. They act as a form of escapism for Cassie, a way to momentarily forget her deeper issues. For the reader, these scenes provide a titillating diversion, steering attention away from Cassie's underlying emotional distress.

While Cassie's life seems like an open book of mishaps and misadventures, there are small, almost imperceptible hints of her deeper turmoil. A throwaway line here, a fleeting thought there – these are the breadcrumbs Fawcett leaves for those willing to look deeper. Cassie's manic behaviour, masked as quirky charm and adoring love, is a symptom of her internal struggle. Yet, it's easy to gloss over these hints when you're caught up in the spectacle of her external life.

Reading *Everything is Perfect* feels like being on a rollercoaster. You're whipped through highs of hilarity and lows of second-hand embarrassment. It's a wild ride that keeps you so entertained you barely have time to catch your breath, let alone ponder the protagonist's mental state. As a reader, you're complicit in the distraction. You want to believe Cassie's life is just a series of funny mishaps and escapades because it's more comfortable than confronting the reality of her situation.

The supporting characters in the novel also play a crucial role in maintaining the illusion. Cassie's friends and love interests are depicted as colourful, larger-than-life personalities who are almost caricatures, initially depicted as oblivious to her deeper issues. They act as mirrors, reflecting the surface-level chaos of her life while ignoring the cracks beneath. This mirroring effect reinforces the reader's perception of Cassie's life as an amusing disaster rather than a cry for help.

When Fawcett finally pulls back the curtain on Cassie's inner turmoil, it's a gut punch. You realise that all the humour and horniness were a smokescreen, obscuring the protagonist's real struggles. Cassie's manic behaviour, previously seen as endearing, now appears in a much darker light. Her cringe-worthy actions are desperate attempts to maintain a facade of normalcy. The reveal is devastating precisely because it feels like a blindside. You were so entangled in her facade that you didn't see the tears.

This is exemplified by the regular ignored phonecalls from her mothers hospital. The contrast between her comedic perceptions and her lonely, despairing solitude that is constantly pushed to the back of her mind, is stark. Eventually it all comes to a head, clutching a bottle of wine and crying uncontrollably, the weight of her struggles and identity becomes undeniable. This scene, stripped of all humour, forces both Cassie and the reader to confront the reality of her situation.

As a reader, this revelation forced me to re-evaluate everything I thought I knew about Cassie. I felt a mix of emotions: guilt for not seeing the signs, sympathy for her struggle, and admiration for Fawcett's storytelling prowess. The experience is both humbling and enlightening. It's a reminder that everyone has hidden depths, and what we see on the surface is often only a fraction of the whole story.

The distraction mirrors how we often deal with mental health in real life. We live in a world full of distractions, (entertainment, work, relationships) all of which can serve to mask our deeper issues. Just as Cassie's antics and romantic escapades distract both her and the reader from her inner turmoil, we often use external distractions to avoid facing our own mental health struggles.

In both fiction and reality, maintaining the illusion of normalcy can be a coping mechanism. Cassie's life, with its endless series of mishaps and romantic entanglements, is a carefully constructed facade. It's easier to laugh off a wardrobe malfunction or a disastrous date than to confront the painful truth of her mental health issues. In real life, we often hide struggles behind a veneer of humour and busyness. They might be the life of the party, the joker in the group, or the overachiever at work, all while battling unseen demons.

Constant distraction comes at a cost. By focusing on the surface-level chaos, we miss the opportunity to address the underlying issues. Cassie's manic behaviour and emotional distress escalate throughout the novel. Culminating in a breakdown that could have been mitigated if she had acknowledged her struggles earlier, and accepted help sooner. This parallels the real-life consequences of ignoring mental health issues. Without proper attention and care, these issues can worsen, leading to more severe outcomes.

Fawcett's novel ultimately suggests that breaking the cycle of distraction and confronting our inner turmoil is essential for healing. Cassie's journey, while painful, is also a path towards self-awareness and recovery. By the end of the novel, she begins to address her mental health issues head-on, seeking help and making changes to be true to herself. This mirrors the real-life process of recognising and addressing mental health struggles. It's a difficult but necessary step towards genuine well-being.

Maxine Fawcett's *Everything is Perfect* is a testament to the power of distraction in storytelling. By keeping readers focused on Cassie's cringe-worthy and horny actions, Fawcett effectively obscures the protagonist's deeper emotional stress and manic behaviours. The narrative techniques she employs are not just clever but deeply impactful, creating a reading experience that aligns you to the same perceptions of its main character.

In the end, *Everything is Perfect* is a powerful exploration of the human condition, wrapped in a deceptively light-hearted package. It's a reminder that beneath the surface of every seemingly perfect life lies a complex web of emotions, struggles, and unspoken truths. And it's a testament to the skill of an author who can make you laugh, cringe, and cry. Sometimes all at once.

28

The Silent Backbone: How Sokka's Wit Shapes Avatar

Sokka from "Avatar: The Last Airbender" serves as a quintessential example of the "ordinary" hero, a beacon for anyone who's ever felt overshadowed in a world of specialists. Unlike his magically endowed peers, Sokka wields no bending powers. Instead, his strengths lie in his sharp wit, inventive mind, and strategic thinking.

The Overlooked Value of the Ordinary

Sokka's contributions, primarily non-physical and based on intellect, are akin to the support beams of a building, essential yet invisible. His ability to anticipate the enemy's movements, devise elaborate plans, and sometimes improvise on the fly showcases a different kind of strength. This intellectual agility points to an important societal truth: the thinkers, planners, and problem-solvers hold our communities together, much like Sokka does with Team Avatar.

In everyday life, we see such roles in the individuals who manage logistics, maintain schedules, and ensure efficiency. Tasks that while crucial, rarely receive the limelight. These roles might not come with grandeur or the awe associated with more visible positions, yet they are fundamental to the success of any organisation or endeavor. They ensure that the machine operates smoothly, that the cogs turn without friction. This metaphorical symphony, orchestrated by those like Sokka, might not make sound, but it creates harmony.

Sokka's experience also resonates deeply with the common feeling of ordinariness, especially in a society that often celebrates overt achievements and easily quantifiable successes. In a team where others wield elemental powers, Sokka initially struggles with feeling out of place. A sentiment mirrored in our own world where the accomplishments of others can sometimes seem to diminish our own.

This feeling is often exacerbated by the modern propensity to compare ourselves with those around us. Social media, professional networking platforms, and even casual conversations can turn into arenas of comparison, where everyone else's highlights make our everyday contributions feel less significant. Sokka's development from feeling like an outsider to recognising his own crucial role within the group serves as a powerful counter-narrative to this pervasive issue.

Acknowledging the importance of these roles can help combat feelings of imposter syndrome and worthlessness. It reminds us that every role contributes to the larger picture, and the absence of one (even the seemingly minor ones) would diminish the whole. Just as a symphony would falter without the conductor, teams falter without their strategists, their thinkers, their Sokkas.

Sokka is Funny

The challenges faced by Team Avatar are immense, from facing powerful enemies to dealing with personal losses. In these high-pressure scenarios, Sokka's humor emerges not just as a relief but as a crucial coping mechanism. It lightens the mood, sure, but more significantly, it helps the team manage stress and anxiety. Humor has the power to put problems into perspective, to make them seem more manageable. It reminds everyone that there is still hope, and joy to be found even when the odds are stacked against them.

Research in psychology supports this idea, humor can reduce the physiological effects of stress and help in maintaining mental health. When Sokka cracks a joke, he's helping stabilise their emotional state, reinforcing their resilience, and ensuring they have the emotional bandwidth to face their next challenge.

Humor also plays a critical role in strengthening social bonds. Shared laughter can promote a sense of unity and trust, creating an environment where members feel more connected and supported. For Team Avatar, every chuckle shared in the heat of a challenge acts like a reaffirmation of their bond. It says, "We're in this together," and "We can face this as long as we don't lose ourselves along the way."

This function of humor is particularly vital in diverse groups, where differences might otherwise drive wedges. Sokka's comedic timing often serves to bridge gaps between the characters, softening moments of tension and misunderstanding. It's a subtle yet powerful reminder that humor can serve as a universal language, capable of bringing people together irrespective of their backgrounds or personal struggles.

Humor serves a deeper, more existential purpose. In the midst of their mission to save the world, it's easy for Aang and the others to lose sight of their own youth, their right to simply be teenagers. Sokka's jokes and pranks remind them (and the audience) that despite the enormity of their responsibilities, they are allowed moments of levity. They are allowed to not take themselves too seriously all the time.

Humor is profoundly significant in real life as well. In the face of personal and global adversities, finding moments for laughter can be a profound assertion of our humanity. It's a way of saying that despite the chaos and threats surrounding us, our spirit, our joy, and our ability to laugh will not be so easily defeated.

Sokka as a leader

Sokka's leadership style, deeply rooted in his emotional intelligence, demonstrates an often underappreciated aspect of effective leadership. Unlike the traditional heroic figure who might lead with sheer force or awe-inspiring skill, Sokka brings a different set of tools to the table: his acute awareness of and responsiveness to the emotions of others.

Emotional intelligence, the ability to identify, understand, and manage emotions, serves as Sokka's compass in navigating the interpersonal dynamics of Team Avatar. This skill set enables him to detect underlying tensions and address them before they escalate, maintaining morale and ensuring that everyone feels heard and valued. For instance, when conflicts arise between Toph and Katara, Sokka often steps in not only with humor to defuse tension but also with empathy to understand each side's perspective. This ability to mediate and maintain peace is crucial for any leader tasked with keeping a group focused and cohesive on common goals.

Sokka's humor, paired with his emotional intelligence, is particularly effective because it is often tailored to the needs of his teammates. He knows when a situation calls for lightening the mood or when a more serious, empathetic approach is needed. This adaptability in leadership is akin to a chef knowing just the right amount of seasoning to add; too much or too little can change the entire dish. In Sokka's case, his 'seasoning' helps maintain a healthy emotional balance within the group, which is essential for their resilience and continued cooperation.

Emotionally intelligent leadership extends beyond just keeping the peace. By managing emotions effectively, he fosters a sense of security and belonging among the team members. This not only enhances individual performance but also deepens the bonds within the team, creating a more profound sense of loyalty and commitment to the group's objectives. In a broader societal context, leaders like Sokka demonstrate the value of emotional intelligence in any collective endeavor, be it in a family, a workplace, or a community group. The stability and harmony he cultivates are testament to the power of understanding and managing emotions effectively.

An Ordinary Inspiration

Sokka's humor and leadership offer more than just comic relief and tactical guidance; they provide a model for impactful contribution through seemingly ordinary skills. His ability to read the room, make strategic decisions, and bring people together are qualities that inspire non-benders to recognise and harness their own unique skills. Sokka demonstrates that these abilities are not just supplementary but are often the linchpin in many of Team Avatar's successes.

Sokka's emotional intelligence highlights a form of inner strength that is accessible to everyone, bender or not. It emphasises that understanding and empathising with others can lead to influential leadership that is as impactful as any display of bending. In this way, Sokka inspires individuals to look beyond traditional metrics of power or talent, valuing instead the quieter, impactful traits that contribute to group dynamics and achievements.

For viewers dealing with feelings of inadequacy or invisibility, Sokka provides a template for harnessing one's unique gifts, whatever they may be. His character proves that you don't need to bend fire or move mountains to change the world; sometimes, making your friends laugh, planning the next step, or simply being there for someone is just as transformative.

Sokka's is a beautifully crafted lesson in the importance of recognising and valuing one's intrinsic worth. In a society that often celebrates only the most apparent achievements (like bending elements or having prestigious titles) Sokka teaches us that the seemingly ordinary individuals often have the most extraordinary impacts. His journey is a comforting beacon for anyone battling feelings of inadequacy, proving that every individual plays a pivotal role in the greater narrative of life, just as Sokka does in his.

29

Dune's Realpolitik of Religion

Dune dishes out its messiah with a spice-laden twist, seasoning it with comparisons to the more grounded, earthy flavors of messianic figures in historical and biblical films. To spice things up, we'll sprinkle in some insights on the recipe adjustments made to characters like Chani and Stilgar from book to film, and marinate it all in the cultural and historical broth that influenced Dune.

The Spice of Life: Paul Atreides vs. Historical Messiahs

Paul Atreides emerges not merely as a leader destined for greatness but as a messiah intricately woven into the fabric of Fremen society. This portrayal starkly diverges from the divine-centric narratives of messiahs in historical and biblical contexts, where figures like Jesus and Moses are depicted as conduits of the divine, performing miracles and imparting wisdom that transcend the mundane realities of their worlds. Instead, Paul's journey to messiahship is deeply rooted in the tangible: the politics, the ecological strife of Arrakis, and (most notably) the spice that defines the planet's very existence. This pivot from the ethereal to the empirical in Dune's narrative reflects a broader thematic exploration, positioning its religious elements as outcomes of practical, historical forces rather than purely divine intervention.

The Bene Gesserit's long-game strategy of gene manipulation and prophecy seeding across galaxies offers a compelling parallel to the pragmatic aspects of religion's spread on Earth. Just as these spacefaring nuns engineer the sociopolitical landscape to herald Paul's coming, real-world religions have historically used strategic missionary work and the adaptation of local customs to embed their teachings within diverse cultures. This methodical approach to cultivating a base of belief underscores a shared understanding: both in the universe of Dune and on our own planet, religion often roots in strategic human action as much as in the spiritual or divine.

Moreover, Paul's ascendancy is inseparable from the socio-political and environmental tapestry of Arrakis, echoing the way earthly messianic figures have risen in response to societal crises. Like Jesus, who preached salvation amid Roman oppression, or Muhammad, who united fragmented tribes with a new religious doctrine, Paul represents a beacon of hope against the backdrop of Arrakis' ecological devastation and imperial tyranny. This confluence of messiahship with the material challenges of the day suggests that Dune, while fantastical, mirrors the intricate dance between religion, politics, and ecology familiar to our world. By grounding its messianic narrative in the realpolitik and environmental struggles of Arrakis, Dune not only differentiates itself from traditional messianic tales but also reflects a nuanced understanding of how religions, and their saviors are often shaped by the earthly realms they seek to transform.

A Tale of Two Characters: Chani and Stilgar's multifaceted zealotry

The film adaptation introduces nuanced shifts in the portrayal of Chani and Stilgar when compared to the novel. These significantly impact the exploration of religion, sacrifice, and zealotry within the context of Paul's rise as a messiah. These character modifications provide a sharper lens through which to view the themes central to the Dune saga.

In the books, Stilgar is depicted as a wise and pragmatic leader, deeply rooted in Fremen traditions yet open to change when it benefits his people. The film, however, recasts Stilgar in a light that emphasises his zealotry and willingness to sacrifice for the cause Paul represents. A striking example is his unwavering support for Paul's jihad, depicted in a scene where Stilgar offers his own life so Paul can speak with Freman leaders, demonstrating a fanaticism and zealotry for Paul's vision. This contrasts with the book, where his concerns about the implications of Paul's war are more pronounced. The film's portrayal underscores a theme of zealotry, showing how the belief in a messiah can drive individuals to extreme actions, echoing real-world instances where religious fervor has led to conflicts justified by faith.

Chani's character undergoes a radical transformation in the film, becoming a vocal critic of Paul's ascendancy to messianic status and the religion forming around him. This is a departure from the softer approach she exhibits in the books regarding Paul's religious role. This shift is exemplified when Chani refuses to bow to Paul, expressing her fears that the burgeoning cult of personality will lead to irreversible changes in Fremen culture, the loss of their identity, and lives. Her opposition to Paul's deification and the blind faith of the followers adds a layer of internal conflict, enriching the narrative with themes of skepticism towards religious authority. Chani's stance introduces a critical viewpoint on the dangers of messianic movements, reflecting real-world tensions between personal belief systems and organised religion.

These character shifts from the source material to the film adaptation profoundly affect the portrayal of religion, sacrifice, and zealotry in Dune Part 2. Stilgar's transformation into a zealot who readily embraces the sacrificial nature of a religious war underlines the dark sides of messianic movements, where belief can sometimes overshadow reason. On the other hand, Chani's opposition to Paul's religious elevation introduces a narrative of resistance to blind faith, emphasising the value of questioning and the potential pitfalls of religious fanaticism.

Together, these character arcs enhance the narrative's exploration of the complexities of faith and leadership. Stilgar's zealotry and Chani's skepticism serve as two sides of the same coin, acting as opposing foils for Paul, presenting the audience with a multifaceted view of the consequences, both positive and negative, of messianic leadership. Through these characters, Dune Part 2 navigates the delicate balance between faith and fanaticism, sacrifice and survival, echoing the intricate dance of religion and power in the real world.

In sum, while the messiahs of history offer us a window into the divine, Dune Part 2 opens a door to a universe where spirituality, politics, and the practicalities of messianism blend into a heady mix, challenging us to rethink what it means to be a savior in a complex and multifaceted world.

30

Treasure Planet: How a Trip to Space Saved an Old Story from Sinking

If Disney had played Treasure Island straight (galleons, grog, eyepatches, and all) we would've politely nodded, maybe watched it on a sleepy Sunday, and then forgotten and discarded like an empty bottle of rum. But Treasure Planet? By jettisoning the sea for the stars it became a classic that permanently occupies a back water system in my brain. It takes Robert Louis Stevenson's classic tale and flings it into space helping it escape the gravity and burden of outdated metaphors. That's not just a cosmetic upgrade. It's the key to why the movie works.

Treasure Island was always a story about venturing into the unknown, breaking away from the dull grind of everyday life, and finding your identity somewhere between a map and a mutiny. In 1883, that unknown was the sea: vast, lawless, full of mystery, and danger. But in 2002, the ocean didn't feel like a wild frontier. It's more of a place for grandparents to take cruises through. Every inch is mapped and triangulated. The idea of sailing into uncharted waters feels less like a thrill and more like a Wi-Fi dead zone.

Instead, Disney swapped oceans for galaxies. And it works because space is the new sea. It has the same infinite possibility, the same potential for lawlessness and wonder, but with the added bonus of being actually unknown to modern viewers. Where 18th-century readers dreamed of unexplored islands, kids today dream about undiscovered planets. Setting the story in space does exactly what the original did for its time. It gives its audience a place to dream about. A place where adventure still feels possible.

This isn't just a cool aesthetic flex (although solar-powered pirate ships with glowing sails are undeniably cool, like, "tattoo this on my soul" cool). The cosmic setting updates the themes. Jim Hawkins isn't just navigating through a chartless quadrant of space, he's navigating that hormone-drenched emotional asteroid field known as adolescence. The metaphor lands harder in zero-G. Space, unlike the ocean, still feels dangerous and exhilarating to us. It's the perfect backdrop for Jim's internal coming-of-age saga.

Then there's the scale. We're talking galactic distances, which only make the story's emotional core more intimate. The bond between Jim and Silver works in any setting, but when you place it against the immensity of the universe, it suddenly has gravity (pun intended). These two could be lightyears apart in age, goals, and cybernetic enhancements, but they form a real connection. That contrast between massive scope and personal closeness makes their relationship hit harder. It's the classic "tiny flame in a vast void" trope, and the increased scale makes it hit even harder.

Now, let's not pretend every change was some deep thematic upgrade. Silver being a cyborg instead of a crusty old pirate? That's just cool. Morph the squishy shape-shifting pet? Comic relief jelly. But those touches add charm, not just noise. They give the animators room to play, to inject the movie with humor and whimsy that a more grounded adaptation might miss. And that matters, too. A story about betrayal, trust, and self-discovery doesn't have to be grim. Sometimes it can be wrapped in laser blasts, neon, and a little goo-creature that turns into a sock.

Treasure Planet doesn't just retell Treasure Island, it retools it. It asks what the original story meant to its readers back then: adventure, mystery, escape, and reimagines where those dreams live today. Not on the waves, but among the stars. Space isn't just a setting here. It's a symbol, a narrative device, and honestly, a giant excuse to make badass art of flying pirate ships. And it works. It makes the story feel fresh, relevant, and unforgettable in a way a straightforward adaptation never could.

31

Arrival and "Not Actually That Deep" Sci-Fi Films

Some science fiction films pull you in, not by spinning tales of intergalactic wars or sprawling alien empires, but by folding reality in on itself like an origami swan. Movies like *Arrival* (2016), *Interstellar*, and *Inception* fall into a genre I lovingly call "not actually that deep sci-fi." Don't get me wrong; this isn't a jab at their quality. It's a compliment. These movies are brilliant precisely because they take complex scientific concepts, wrap them in mind-bending narratives, and make you question everything, for about a second. Until you walk away feeling entertained, not overwhelmed. Let's unpack this with *Arrival* as our centerpiece, then take a look at how it stacks up against its high-concept sci-fi cousins.

Arrival is a masterpiece of restrained storytelling. It's a movie about alien linguistics, non-linear time, and the weight of communication. Sounds heavy, right? But it isn't bogged down in dense, existential philosophy. It's sleek, compelling, and leaves you marveling at the beauty of its ideas rather than their inscrutability.

Here's the gist: Aliens land on Earth, but instead of threatening to blow us up, they offer the ultimate gift, language. However, their language isn't your standard Rosetta Stone fare. It's circular, infinite, and shifts your perception of time itself. Louise Banks, played by Amy Adams, learns this alien tongue, and with it, she starts seeing her life as a whole. Past, present, and future all at once. The result? A stunning twist where we realise her grief for her future daughter has already been experienced, yet she chooses to embrace the joy and sorrow of that life anyway.

The science checks out enough to keep the audience on board, and that's where *Arrival* shines. The concept of language shaping cognition is grounded in the Sapir-Whorf hypothesis, a real linguistic theory. Non-linear time is a brain-bending idea for most of us, but the movie simplifies it to an emotional core: Would you choose pain if it came packaged with joy? The beauty is in its simplicity.

Movies like *Arrival* thrive because they are about science, not scientists. They don't lose the audience in technical jargon or spend hours explaining the mechanics of wormholes or non-linear time. Instead, they present these ideas like a magician pulling a rabbit out of a hat: confidently, with just enough explanation to make it feel real. You don't need to know how the trick works to appreciate it.

Take *Interstellar*. It's ostensibly about love and space travel, but its real showstopper is the depiction of gravity and time dilation. That scene where Matthew McConaughey's character realises that hours on one planet equate to decades back on Earth is emotionally gutting and scientifically accurate (to a point). Like *Arrival*, it uses a scientific concept to drive the story forward while making you gasp at the implications.

Similarly, *Inception* toys with the layers of dreams within dreams. The "is it real or isn't it?" ending doesn't fundamentally change the plot but makes you reconsider what you've just seen. It's not about fully understanding the mechanics of dream-sharing technology; it's about the personal stakes. The science is window dressing for a great character-driven story.

These films take science and concepts that are just close enough to reality to feel plausible, grounding the audience in familiarity before nudging them into the extraordinary. *The Martian*, for instance, fits into this realm but skews less mind-bending. Its core concept, 'how do you survive alone on Mars?' Is a more practical question than "how does time dilate on a massive spinning black hole?" Its strength lies in realism, and while it's fascinating, it lacks the reality-warping edge of *Arrival* or *Interstellar*.

The "mind-bending" concepts in these movies aren't that mind-bending if you've spent any time researching or learning scientific theories. Non-linear time? Sure, Einstein's theories of relativity hint at similar ideas. Wormholes? A staple of speculative physics. The real trick is that these films don't pretend these concepts are the point of the story. Instead, they use them to create emotional stakes and compelling narratives.

That's what makes them so effective. They hint at the trippier implications of their ideas, *Inception's* layers of simulation, *Arrival's* circular time, but they don't linger there. They're about the human experience: grief, love, survival, and the choices we make.

Compare that to *The Matrix*, which is more about its concept than its execution. It's a fantastic movie, but its focus on simulated reality as a philosophical dilemma puts it in a different category. It doesn't aim for realism or plausibility; it's all about the spectacle.

Ultimately, movies like *Arrival* succeed because they make high-concept ideas accessible. They're like a rollercoaster for your brain: thrilling, surprising, and expertly engineered. They don't demand you read up on quantum physics to enjoy them. Instead, they trust their audiences to suspend disbelief and ride along.

For those of us who love science and science fiction, these films are the perfect middle ground. They represent scientific concepts well enough to be satisfying, without drowning us in technicalities. So yeah, they might not shatter your worldview or change your life, but they will make you say, "Whoa, that's cool," which is often exactly what we want from a movie.

32

Grounding Fantasy: Lessons from Delicious in Dungeon

In the sprawling landscape of fantasy, where dragons soar and magic crackles through the air, the most captivating elements often lie in the small, relatable moments. Enter "Delicious in Dungeon," a manga-turned-anime that brilliantly roots its fantastical world in the most mundane of human activities: cooking and eating. This essay explores how the show's focus on these everyday activities makes its fantasy world more relatable and grounded, comparing its approach to other fantasy shows and their methods of grounding their worlds. Additionally, it delves into how this technique can be applied to other genres and examines other grounding techniques that enhance the relatability of fantasy settings.

"Delicious in Dungeon" begins with a classic fantasy premise: a group of adventurers delving into a dungeon. However, instead of merely hacking and slashing their way through, they face a more immediate and relatable challenge: hunger. The group decides to cook and eat the monsters they encounter, turning survival into a culinary adventure. This focus on cooking and eating does more than fill the adventurers' bellies; it fills the world with life. Food is a universal experience, something that every viewer can relate to. By integrating it into the core of the story, "Delicious in Dungeon" makes

GROUNDING FANTASY: LESSONS FROM DELICIOUS IN DUNGEON

its fantastical setting feel tangible and real. The characters' interactions with food reveal their personalities, strengths, and weaknesses in a way that traditional combat scenes often do not.

The worldbuilding is where the show truly shines. Each episode introduces new creatures and plants, with detailed explanations of their habitats and characteristics, often tying them back to real-world analogs. This method allows viewers to quickly grasp the world's complexity through familiar concepts. For example, the show starts with simple hunting scenes, where characters discuss the edibility and flavor of various monsters. As the series progresses, it delves deeper into the world's ecosystems, farming, conflict, and even philosophies all through the lens of food. Each new discovery is linked to the characters' immediate need for sustenance, creating a natural flow of information that feels both educational and entertaining.

This gradual rollout of world complexity through food interactions is a masterstroke. It mirrors how we learn about our own world: through everyday experiences and necessities. The tools used for cooking also reveal insights into the world's technology and craftsmanship. A pot made of rare metal, alludes to the greater world's materials, building images of what is beyond our immediate story.

One of the most striking aspects of "Delicious in Dungeon" is how it makes the viewer care about the minutiae of daily life in a fantasy setting. Cooking scenes are depicted with meticulous attention to detail, from the preparation of ingredients to the final presentation of the dish. This level of detail not only makes the food look mouth-watering but also emphasises the importance of these small moments. Consider how the show handles secondary ingredients and spices. In many fantasy worlds, these would be glossed over or replaced with magical equivalents. However, "Delicious in Dungeon" treats them with the same reverence as any other crucial plot point. The discovery of a new ingredient can lead to moments of joy and bonding among the characters, reminding viewers of their own experiences with food.

Cooking and eating together fosters a sense of community and shared responsibility among the characters. These scenes offer a glimpse into their daily lives, showing how they cooperate and support each other. It's in these moments that their personalities shine through—whether it's the meticulous preparation by the dwarf Senshi or the enthusiastic experimentation by the main protagonist, Laios. This focus on shared responsibility grounds the characters and makes their world more relatable. In many fantasy shows, characters are often depicted as lone heroes or isolated figures. "Delicious in Dungeon" breaks this mould by emphasising the importance of teamwork and collaboration, not just in battle, but in everyday survival.

To fully appreciate the unique approach of "Delicious in Dungeon," it's helpful to compare it with other fantasy shows and their methods of grounding their worlds. Many fantasy series rely on grandiose settings, epic battles, and complex political intrigue to create a sense of realism and depth. While effective, these methods can sometimes distance the viewer from the characters' everyday experiences.

In "Game of Thrones," the intricate political plots and vast landscapes create a rich and immersive world. However, the focus is often on the larger-than-life conflicts and power struggles, leaving little room for the mundane aspects of life. Similarly, "The Lord of the Rings" builds its world through epic quests and detailed lore, but the daily lives of its characters are mostly glossed over.

In contrast, "Delicious in Dungeon" grounds its fantasy world in the everyday act of cooking and eating. This approach makes the characters more relatable and their world more accessible. It's not just about the grand adventure; it's about how they survive and thrive in their environment. By focusing on the micro rather than the macro, the show creates a more intimate and engaging experience for the viewer.

There's something deeply human about food and cooking. It brings people together in ways few other activities can. This universality is what makes

GROUNDING FANTASY: LESSONS FROM DELICIOUS IN DUNGEON

"Delicious in Dungeon" so effective in grounding its fantasy world. No matter how fantastical the setting, the act of preparing and sharing a meal is something everyone can understand and appreciate. It reminds us that fantasy worlds don't need to be grounded solely through epic battles or complex lore. Sometimes, the most powerful way to make a world feel real is through the simple, everyday activities that connect us all. By focusing on food and cooking, the show taps into a fundamental aspect of human experience, making its fantasy world not only more relatable but also more memorable.

The success of "Delicious in Dungeon" in grounding its fantasy world through cooking and eating raises an interesting question: How can similar grounding techniques be applied to other genres? The core idea is to find universal, relatable elements that can anchor a story, making even the most fantastical or abstract settings feel tangible and real.

In science fiction, grounding techniques can involve focusing on the mundane aspects of futuristic life. For instance, exploring how characters in a space colony handle everyday tasks like maintaining their habitats, dealing with limited resources, or even social interactions in confined spaces can add depth and relatability. "The Expanse" does this well by showing the daily struggles of life in space, from water scarcity to the effects of low gravity on the human body.

In romance, grounding often comes through the exploration of everyday relationship dynamics. Instead of relying solely on grand romantic gestures, stories can delve into the small, intimate moments that define relationships: shared routines, personal quirks, and the challenges of everyday life together. The TV series "Normal People" exemplifies this by focusing on the nuanced, evolving relationship between its main characters, highlighting both their emotional highs and mundane interactions.

Grounding in historical fiction can involve meticulous attention to the daily lives and cultural practices of the time period. By focusing on how characters navigate their everyday environments, authors can create a vivid, immersive experience that brings history to life. Hilary Mantel's "Wolf Hall" series, for example, brings the Tudor court to life through detailed descriptions of the characters' daily routines, clothing, and social customs.

While "Delicious in Dungeon" uses food and cooking to ground its fantasy world, there are numerous other techniques that writers can employ to achieve similar effects.One of the most effective grounding techniques is to focus on realistic character interactions. By ensuring that characters react and interact in ways that feel authentic, writers can make their fantasy worlds more relatable. This includes showing characters dealing with everyday emotions and problems, even in the midst of fantastical events.

Another technique is to create detailed, lived-in environments. By describing settings with attention to detail, including sensory details like sounds, smells, and textures, writers can make fantasy worlds feel more real. This can involve everything from the architecture and landscape to the weather and local customs. Incorporating cultural practices and social norms from the real world can also help ground a fantasy setting. This can involve creating fictional festivals, rituals, and traditions that mirror those in our own world. By doing so, writers can create a sense of familiarity and depth, making their worlds feel more lived-in and authentic.

Exploring the economic and political systems of a fantasy world can add a layer of realism and complexity. By showing how characters navigate these systems, whether through trade, governance, or social hierarchy, writers can create a more immersive and believable world. George R.R. Martin's "A Song of Ice and Fire" series excels in this regard, with its intricate political plots and economic realities.

"Delicious in Dungeon" offers a refreshing take on the fantasy genre by grounding its world in the relatable and universal experiences of cooking and eating. Through detailed worldbuilding, shared responsibility, and a focus on the minutiae of daily life, the show creates a rich and immersive world that feels both familiar and fantastical. By comparing this approach to other fantasy shows, we see how "Delicious in Dungeon" stands out in its ability to make the extraordinary feel ordinary and the mundane feel magical.

The grounding techniques used in "Delicious in Dungeon" can be applied across genres, from science fiction to horror, romance, and historical fiction. By focusing on universal, relatable elements, writers can create stories that resonate with audiences on a deeper level. Whether through realistic character interactions, detailed environments, cultural practices, or economic and political systems, grounding techniques add depth and authenticity to any setting.

In the end, it's a testament to the power of food and cooking to connect us all, no matter what world we find ourselves in. It reminds us that the most compelling stories often lie in the small, everyday moments that make us human. By embracing these moments, writers can create rich, relatable worlds that captivate and inspire, making the fantastical feel real and the mundane feel magical.

33

Polishing the Past: Ethical Memoir Writing Explored Through The End of Your Life Book Club

Writing a memoir is like polishing silverware, it's a process that requires delicacy and precision to enhance beauty without causing any scratches. Will Schwalbe's *The End of Your Life Book Club* perfectly illustrates this meticulous craft, offering us a profound glimpse into his journey with his mother during her last days, while he delicately buffs the surface of their shared experiences to reveal a lustrous narrative beneath.

At its heart, a memoir is deeply personal and inherently invasive. The genre demands authenticity and often delves into the intimate details of lives, not just the author's but also those around them. Schwalbe's book is a poignant example. It's not just about his mother's battle with cancer; it's an introspective look at their shared love for books and how those books shaped their final conversations and his mother's legacy. Here, Schwalbe is not just a narrator but also a son, a caretaker, and a reflective observer of a deeply personal and transformative experience.

Schwalbe's memoir navigates the fine line between revealing and concealing, varnishing his mother's story without concealing its essence. Schwalbe discusses his mother's illness, treatments, and even family dynamics. This transparency serves the story and its emotional impact but also risks exposing more than what his mother, were she able to consent posthumously, might have wished.

The key here is consent. While Schwalbe's mother was alive, she was aware of his project and, presumably, her portrayal in it. This mutual understanding between the subject and the storyteller is crucial. For memoirists treading similar paths, maintaining ethical integrity starts with this consent. It's about ensuring that the subjects are comfortable, aware of the portrayal, and, ideally, involved in the narrative process.

Ethical memoir writing extends beyond mere consent; it involves a portrayal that respects the subject's dignity and legacy. Schwalbe's narrative respects his mother's intellect and bravery, crafting a legacy that emphasises her strength and wisdom rather than just her illness. His portrayal evokes empathy and admiration, which suggests ethical lines were navigated successfully.

Memoirists must ask themselves: Are they writing to share a story that needs to be told, or simply to sensationalise personal drama? The intent should be to honour the memories and experiences, not exploit them for dramatic effect. The narrative should aim to preserve and restore, the subject's memory without altering its original character.

Moreover, there's a responsibility toward the reader. A memoirist must navigate the waters of bias and subjectivity. Acknowledging one's perspective as just one angle of the truth helps maintain narrative integrity. Schwalbe does this by focusing on events, but more importantly, the emotional and philosophical reflections they provoke, offering readers a personal restoration to view, not just events but their impacts.

For those looking to embark on writing someone else's story, consider this a gentle reminder: tread lightly and carry the responsibility gracefully. Begin with consent, proceed with respect, and aim for a portrayal that adds depth and dignity to the person's legacy. Remember, you're not just a writer but a steward of someone's history. Just like a well-restored heirloom, a good memoir can illuminate, whereas a poorly handled one can detract from its value.

Schwalbe's memoir is a valuable case study for ethical memoir writing. In weaving the personal with the universal, he sets a precedent for how stories of love, loss, and literature can be told with creativity, candour, and care.

34

The Role of Reader Engagement

Edward de Bono's *Teaching Thinking* is a comprehensive guide that aims to improve our cognitive abilities. Like a treasure map, it provides the routes and landmarks necessary to navigate the complex landscape of thought. The balance between theory and practice, as well as the writing style, plays a significant role in keeping readers engaged. By examining these elements closely, we can uncover the treasure of effective engagement and apply these insights to our own writing.

De Bono starts by establishing a strong theoretical foundation. This section is dense with concepts and frameworks that explain the 'why' behind different thinking strategies. The initial chapters are like the detailed explanations on a treasure map, describing the terrain, climate, and potential challenges one might encounter. They are crucial for understanding the broader context and preparing for the journey ahead.

An overemphasis on theory can be overwhelming. Readers might feel like they are stuck in an endless exposition, waiting for the practical applications that make the theory come alive. This is a common pitfall in instructional writing. The key is to blend theory and practice seamlessly, ensuring that each theoretical concept is immediately followed by a practical example or exercise. This approach not only reinforces the theory but also keeps the reader actively engaged.

In applying this principle to other writing, one should intersperse theoretical discussions with practical applications. For instance, after introducing a new concept, immediately follow it with a real-world example or a case study that illustrates how the concept can be applied. This method helps to break down complex ideas into manageable chunks and keeps the reader's attention focused.

De Bono's writing style in *Teaching Thinking* is clear and structured. Each section is clearly marked with regular subheadings, allowing readers to navigate through the content with ease. This clarity is especially important in instructional writing, as it helps to break down complex ideas into understandable parts.

A segmented approach can also disrupt the flow of the narrative. Just as a treasure map with too many detailed sections can make it difficult to see the overall path, overly segmented writing can make it hard for readers to grasp the bigger picture. De Bono often falls in this camp, at times using subheadings for every paragraph. The challenge is to provide clear and detailed explanations without losing the narrative flow that ties everything together.

To address this in other writings, focus on creating a narrative thread that runs through the entire piece. Even when breaking down the content into smaller sections, ensure that each section naturally leads into the next. It should be possible to remove all subheadings and the piece still flow, then you can choose when to add them back in for clarity. This approach helps to maintain a sense of continuity and makes it easier for readers to follow the overall argument.

To keep readers engaged, it's important to employ strategies that cater to different styles and preferences. De Bono's use of a titling system is one such strategy. By clearly marking each section, he makes it easier for readers to find the information they need and to jump between sections as needed. This approach caters to readers who prefer a more flexible and non-linear reading experience.

The system also has its drawbacks. Just as a treasure map with too many shortcuts can lead to missed landmarks, a book with too many clearly marked sections can encourage readers to skip ahead and miss important information. If too many shortcuts are taken key moments are missed, recurring threads and lost and the impression on the reader is reduced. To counter this, it's important to create a sense of anticipation, value and curiosity that keeps readers moving forward in a linear way, only skipping small sections at a time.

While using clear headings and subheadings to organise the content, also incorporate elements that encourage readers to keep reading. For example, pose a question at the end of a section that is answered in the next, or hint at a particularly interesting case study that is discussed later in the piece. These techniques help to maintain reader interest and encourage a more thorough reading of the content.

One of the key strengths of *Teaching Thinking* is its practical applications. De Bono provides numerous exercises and examples that help to illustrate the theoretical concepts discussed in the book. These practical elements provide tangible rewards for the reader's efforts.

As nuggets of gold, it's important to ensure that these practical elements are well-integrated with the theoretical content. In some cases, the transition from theory to practice can feel abrupt, making it difficult for readers to see the connection between the two. To avoid this, weave practical examples throughout the theoretical discussions, creating a seamless blend of theory and practice. For example, if discussing a particular cognitive strategy, provide a real-world scenario where this strategy can be applied. Also include exercises that readers can try on their own, helping to reinforce the theoretical concepts and providing a more interactive reading experience.

One of the challenges of writing a book like *Teaching Thinking* is creating a cohesive narrative that ties all the concepts together. De Bono's segmented approach, while clear and organised, can sometimes make it difficult to see the overarching themes and connections between different ideas. Just as a cluttered map with too many labeled landmarks can make it hard to see the whole route, a book with too many isolated sections can make it hard to grasp the bigger picture.

To address this, create a narrative thread that runs through the entire book. This thread should tie together the different concepts and provide a sense of continuity and progression. In other writings, focus on creating a clear and compelling narrative that guides readers through the content. Start with a broad overview of the main concepts and themes, and then gradually delve into more detailed discussions, always linking back to the overarching narrative.

For example, if writing about cognitive strategies, start with an introduction that outlines the main themes and goals of the book. Then, break down the content into smaller sections, each focusing on a specific strategy or concept. Throughout these sections, constantly refer back to the main themes and goals, helping to reinforce the overall narrative and create a sense of continuity.

Teaching Thinking is a valuable guide for improving cognitive abilities, and a case study in writing instructional books. Maintaining reader engagement in such a book requires a careful balance of theory and practice, a clear and engaging writing style, and strategies that cater to different preferences. By blending theory and practice seamlessly, maintaining a clear but fluid writing style, and creating a cohesive narrative, writers can ensure that their readers stay engaged and motivated throughout the journey. These principles are not only applicable to de Bono's work but also to any instructional writing, helping to create content that is both informative and engaging.

Drive to Survive: Storytelling Over Speed and Specs
Imagine you're trying to explain Formula 1 to someone who knows nothing

about racing. You could dive into technical jargon about downforce, drag coefficients, and tire degradation... or you could just point to Drive to Survive. Netflix's hit series has made F1 accessible, compelling, and downright addictive by ignoring all the hyper-specialised stuff that insiders obsess over. Instead of getting tangled up in the mechanics of the sport, the show zeroes in on what makes anything captivating, great storytelling.

Chronology? Overrated. Drama? Essential.

At first glance, it seems counterintuitive. A show about a Formula 1 season, where every race builds on the last, and the points tally determines the ultimate winner, shouldn't you, you know, tell it in order? Nope. That's the thinking of someone who cares about keeping the integrity of the spreadsheet, and they're all cowards.

Each episode focuses on a team, a driver, or a specific controversy. It slices up the season into deliciously dramatic chunks, often zooming in on moments that feel earth-shattering for the people involved. The show doesn't care if it has to jump forward two races or back a month to tell the juiciest version of the story. By breaking free from the constraints of a linear timeline, it captures the emotional highs and lows in a way that makes the stakes crystal clear to viewers who might not even know what an apex is.

Think about it: in real life, a mid-season battle between two drivers might feel like a blip in the context of a 23-race calendar. But in Drive to Survive, they'll make it an entire episode, leaning into the rivalry, the pit crew drama, and the inevitable radio message where someone whines, "This is ridiculous!" It's alchemy, taking the chaos of a season and rearranging it to hit the emotional bullseye every time.

The Art of Focus

By zooming in on one team, driver, or figure per episode, the show becomes deeply personal. F1 is a circus of moving parts: 20 drivers, 10 teams, 23 races, and about a million people behind the scenes. Trying to cover all of it at once would be like trying to watch 20 different TV shows simultaneously. Instead, Drive to Survive picks its battles, focusing on a handful of narratives that feel like self-contained dramas within the larger season.

An episode might follow Haas, the scrappy underdog team where things seem to go wrong so consistently you wonder if they've angered some kind of racing deity. Another might zero in on a driver like Daniel Ricciardo, whose megawatt smile hides the simmering frustration of struggling with a car that just won't cooperate. These are short films about ambition, failure, redemption, and sometimes pure pettiness.

The Heart of the Matter: People

Here's the not-so-secret sauce: Drive to Survive makes you care about the people. The show takes larger-than-life figures, like Lewis Hamilton, Max Verstappen, and Toto Wolff, and turns them into fully realised characters. You see them not just as athletes or team principals but as humans grappling with pressure, ego, and the relentless grind of competing at the highest level.

Even better, it shines a spotlight on the unsung heroes and lesser-known players in the F1 world. You don't have to know the difference between a front wing and a rear wing to get why it's heartbreaking when a mechanic stays up all night fixing a car, only to see it crash on lap one. It's not about the nuts and bolts; it's about the people holding the wrenches.

A New Standard

Drive to Survive has set a new bar for documentary storytelling. It's proof that you can take a niche, technical subject and make it universally compelling if you focus on what makes it human. Sure, it helps that Formula 1 is inherently dramatic: fast cars, big egos, and obscene amounts of money; but, the show's success is about more than the subject matter. It's about how you tell the story.

For anyone creating art, documentaries, or even PowerPoint presentations with a million aspects to juggle, Drive to Survive is a masterclass. Forget the specs and the spreadsheets. Start with the story, and everything else will fall into place.

35

The Quiet Revolution: How Thich Nhat Hanh Changed Spiritual Publishing

In the vast, sometimes tumultuous ocean of the publishing industry, where the waves of traditional and modern teaching methods perpetually clash, there floats a serene lotus. The teaching approach of Thich Nhat Hanh. This Zen master, revered for his gentle wisdom, chose a path less traveled, one that has intrigued scholars and practitioners alike. Instead of penning down didactic texts, he turned the essence of his spoken word into written form, an approach that mirrors his teachings on presence, listening, and communication. This essay wades through the waters of Thich Nhat Hanh's communicative teaching methods, using "The Art of Mindful Living" as our compass, to explore how his unique approach compares to the traditional Buddhist teachings, and what this means for the larger publishing industry.

Imagine, sitting under a leafy tree on a crisp morning, the air filled with the sound of Thich Nhat Hanh's voice. His words flow like a gentle stream, reaching not just your ears but the very depths of your soul. This is the experience he sought to replicate in print. By choosing to publish transcriptions of his talks rather than traditional texts, Thich Nhat Hanh invites readers into a space of active engagement, a form of mindful listening that transcends the physical boundaries of time and space. It's akin to having a personal Zen master in your living room, albeit one that doesn't mind if you're in your pajamas and haven't brushed your hair yet.

Traditional Buddhist teachings often come in the form of sutras and commentaries, dense with doctrinal expositions and philosophical musings. While undeniably rich in wisdom, they can sometimes feel like trying to drink from a fire hose. Overwhelming. In contrast, Thich Nhat Hanh's method fosters a more experiential understanding of mindfulness and Zen Buddhism. It's less about gulping down spiritual insights and more about savoring them, one mindful sip at a time. This approach not only makes the teachings more accessible but also embodies the very essence of mindfulness by encouraging a deep, present-moment engagement with the text.

However, no path is without its pebbles. Some might argue that the subtleties of Thich Nhat Hanh's teachings could be lost in transcription. Moreover, the lack of structured exposition and scholarly critique that traditional texts offer might leave some readers craving a more solid ground to stand on. Yet, this seemingly unstructured approach mirrors life itself: messy, unpredictable, and rich with unspoken wisdom waiting to be discovered by those willing to listen deeply.

Thich Nhat Hanh's methods are deeply rooted in the Buddhist tradition of oral teachings. This lineage of wisdom passed down through the ages emphasises the power of spoken word and direct transmission from teacher to student. By embodying this tradition in a modern context, Thich Nhat Hanh bridges the ancient and the contemporary, offering a refreshing alternative in the realm of spiritual literature.

As we drift towards the shores of the publishing industry, it becomes clear that Thich Nhat Hanh's approach is both a gentle breeze and a powerful gust of wind. In a sea of bestsellers clamoring for attention with flashy covers and sensationalist titles, his works stand out in their simplicity and depth. This has undoubtedly contributed to a richer, more diverse publishing landscape, challenging industry norms and encouraging readers and publishers alike to reconsider what constitutes valuable content.

Thich Nhat Hanh's teaching approach, exemplified in "The Art of Mindful Living," offers a profound alternative to traditional Buddhist teaching methods. It's a reminder that in our fast-paced, information-overloaded world, there's immense value in slowing down, listening deeply, and being fully present. As the publishing industry continues to evolve, it's clear that approaches like Thich Nhat Hanh's not only enrich the tapestry of available literature but also guide us toward a more mindful, compassionate way of being in the world.

36

The Enigmatic Cloak of Spiritual Science

In the labyrinth of self-help and spiritual enlightenment, Deepak Chopra's "Reinventing the Body, Resurrecting the Soul" stands as a beacon of promise, offering a path to transformation that bridges the physical with the metaphysical. At first glance, Chopra, with his unique blend of medical expertise and spiritual insight, appears to wield the double-edged sword of science and spirituality with the finesse of a seasoned warrior. However, a closer, more critical examination reveals that this sword may sometimes act more like a magician's wand, using the smoke and mirrors of scientific jargon to dazzle and bewilder the uninitiated. This essay delves into the heart of Chopra's writing, dissecting whether his use of scientific language serves as a foundation of strength or a facade of complexity, and how this reflects broader cultural tendencies in public communication.

Chopra's medical background is undeniable, a credential that imbues his arguments with an aura of credibility. When he speaks, people listen, not just because of what he says, but how he says it. The allure of medical terminology and scientific references in his writing cannot be overstated; they act as a seal of approval, a testament to the rigor and seriousness of his claims. Yet, this reliance on scientific language and concepts can be a double-edged sword. To the untrained ear, terms like "quantum healing," "cellular intelligence," and "neuroplasticity" sound impressive, a reassurance that the author knows what he's talking about. But does this scientific veneer enhance the validity of Chopra's arguments, or does it obscure a lack of substantive evidence?

Critics argue that Chopra's sophisticated use of jargon and medical terminology often crosses into the realm of pseudoscience, using the complexity of language to make arguments seem unassailable. The danger here is not just in misunderstanding, but in the potential to mask weaker arguments behind the formidable shield of scientific respectability. If one digs beneath the surface, the question arises: are these concepts presented with the robust backing of empirical research, or are they speculative, stretched to fit the narrative of spiritual wellness? This tactic, whether intentional or not, can create an "emperor's new clothes" scenario, where to question the science is to admit one's own ignorance.

Yet, to dismiss Chopra's work as mere scientific obfuscation would be to overlook the profound impact it has had on countless individuals seeking healing and transformation. Perhaps the strength of Chopra's writing lies not in the scientific grounding of each claim but in his ability to synthesise complex ideas into a cohesive, compelling vision of wellness. In this light, the use of medical and scientific terminology is not so much a veil to conceal weak arguments but a bridge connecting the realms of modern science and ancient wisdom. Chopra's real accomplishment may be in how he uses his medical background to lend a voice of authority to spiritual practices, thereby elevating their status in a society that often values empirical evidence over experiential knowledge.

In navigating through the dense forest of Deepak Chopra's "Reinventing the Body, Resurrecting the Soul," we encounter a complex interplay between the scientific and the spiritual, a dance of words that both enlightens and obscures. The crux of the matter lies in discerning whether Chopra's liberal sprinkling of scientific terminology acts as a smokescreen, cleverly designed to mask less substantiated arguments, or if it genuinely serves to deepen our understanding of his spiritual teachings.

Upon closer examination, it becomes evident that Chopra's use of jargon, while at times verging on the esoteric, does more than merely dazzle with linguistic pyrotechnics. It acts as a bridge, connecting two worlds that have long been estranged: the empirical realm of science and the intuitive domain of spirituality. This fusion, albeit complex and sometimes bewildering, challenges us to expand our frames of reference, to see beyond the limitations of conventional scientific inquiry and embrace a more holistic view of existence. In this light, the scientific terminology employed by Chopra does not obscure but enriches, offering a multidimensional perspective that invites deeper reflection and understanding.

However, this is not to say that Chopra's approach is without its pitfalls. The very complexity that adds depth can also alienate or confuse readers not versed in the nuanced language of quantum physics or neuroscience. It is here, in the balance between enlightenment and obfuscation, that Chopra's skill as a communicator is truly tested. By weaving scientific concepts into the fabric of spiritual exploration, he challenges us to question and expand our understanding, but the responsibility rests with us, the readers, to navigate these waters with a critical eye. We must sift through the jargon, discerning between genuine insight and speculative extrapolation, between the depth of wisdom and the dazzle of words.

In conclusion, Deepak Chopra's work embodies a daring attempt to reconcile the seemingly disparate worlds of science and spirituality. While his use of scientific terminology may at times feel overwhelming, it ultimately serves to add depth and complexity to his spiritual teachings. This approach not only reflects Chopra's deep respect for the scientific method but also his commitment to a more integrated, holistic view of human well-being. In a broader cultural context, Chopra's synthesis of science and spirituality echoes a growing desire to transcend traditional boundaries of knowledge and understanding, inviting us into a more nuanced and expansive exploration of our existence. As we grapple with the challenges of navigating the information age, Chopra's work stands as a testament to the power of language to both reveal and transform, urging us toward a deeper, more integrated understanding of ourselves and the world around us.

About the Author

Three lenses shape Joseph's work. Writing practice guides structure, clarity, and pace. Board game design brings attention to systems, incentives, and fair play. Learning design keeps the takeaways practical. Together they led to essays that point at a moment, explain the move, and show what it changed.

On the page, Joseph favors short sections, concrete examples, and visible sources. References point to exact timecodes or pages when possible. The pieces keep context tight and skip plot dumps. A chapter on heist pilots looks at how early promises set stakes. A scene study from The Leftovers checks how knowledge flows between character and viewer.

Playtesting shaped the format. Joseph builds a small thing that works end to end, tries it with real readers, then trims steps and labels the confusing parts. That is why essays end with a frame, a prompt, or a short list you can use on your next watch or read. The tools are small on purpose. They help people see and talk about a choice without turning it into homework.

He writes for readers who enjoy media and want a clearer view without extra jargon. He also writes for teachers, facilitators, and designers who need fresh prompts tied to real examples. The aim is a better time with the media you already like and a cleaner way to explain why a moment works.

Joseph works at the overlap of story and systems. He publishes on his site, mentors writers and designers, and supports teams that need clearer rulebooks, stronger playtests, or practical workshop kits. He has worked with small startups and large departments in tech, education, and nonprofits. The through line is simple tools, real users, and results that last after handover.

Thank you for reading. If a piece helped you see a scene more clearly, share it. If a frame helped you run a discussion, reuse it. If a checklist helped you spot a craft move, try it again on a different title. The tools in this book are meant to travel.

You can connect with me on:
- https://opinionatedomanyte.wixsite.com/akis-amusements
- https://www.linkedin.com/in/joseph-atkinson-7b8a2b183

www.ingramcontent.com/pod-product-compliance
Lightning Source LLC
Chambersburg PA
CBHW060401080526
44583CB00012B/417